everyone's a
GENIUS

"Everyone is a genius. But if you judge
a fish on its ability to climb a tree,
it will live its whole life believing it is stupid."
- attributed to Albert Einstein

─────────────────

"Everyone is born a genius, but the process
of life de-geniuses them."
- R. Buckminster Fuller

─────────────────

"Everyone is a genius at least once a year.
The real geniuses simply have their
bright ideas closer together."
- G. C. Lichtenberg

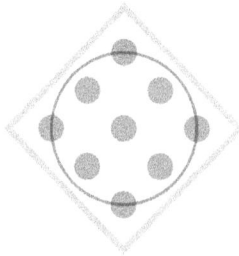

Axiom Business Book Awards
Silver Winner, Business Reference Book, 2015.

Shelf Unbound - Notable 100 Book, 2015.

Bookdesigner.com - Best non-fiction
book cover design, April 2015.

Indie Book of the Day - 2 June 2015.

"Inspired, generous and filled to the brim with action--your action. Go!"

- Seth Godin, Author, 'The Icarus Deception'

"I read *'Everyone's a Genius'* and it sparked a rambling 1,800 word commentary. It's a rare book that sets me off like this."

- Piers Anthony, New York Times Best Selling Author

"One Of The Best Books I Have Ever Read.
Every high school and college student should have to write a report on this book so that they don't wake up late in life in that ah-ha moment wondering what the heck happened to the life that they were given."

- Professor H, Top 50 Amazon Reviewer

"Very few people.. are intelligent enough to explain even simple theories. Fraser has the gift of explaining it simply."

- Graham H. Seibert, Amazon Reviewer

"Honest, realistic and, above all else, true... often brutally so.
Jen pulls no punches. Listen to her, not the dream-stealers."

- Kevin Zwierzchaczewski, Singer & Songwriter, London, UK

"The writing is crisp and engaging... Although *'Everyone's a Genius'* can be read in an afternoon or evening, its message will inspire you for a lifetime."

- Doug Erlandson, Top 50 Amazon Reviewer

"Five out of five! This is a highly enjoyable and beautifully illustrated book, which will help you discover you're capable of so much more than you'd believe. It's already sparked off a few ideas in me for the future."

– Dr Nik Whitehead, Lecturer, University of Wales Trinity St David, Swansea, UK

"This book is a gem! Few are as entertaining, practical and immensely readable as this book. If you are serious about wanting that BIG idea that will change your life, this is the book for you."

– Michael Michalko, internationally acclaimed creativity expert and best-selling author of 'Thinkertoys'

"The perfect introduction to innovation and creativity, this book is not only filled with wonderful illustrations, it also sizzles with inspiration to take your idea and nurture it into a living thing."

– Steve Bynon, Innovation and Enterprise Manager, Mind, Bexley, UK

"Jen Fraser summarises the essential concepts of creating the future you may not even know you can achieve. Read this book, apply it to your life, claim the future you deserve. It's that simple!"

– Paul Adams, President, Queensland Shakespeare Ensemble, Australia

"This book will help you shortcut past the theory and get right to the act of thinking deeply, leveraging your imagination and solving real problems. Now you can put your creative mind to use... immediately!"

– Paul R. Williams, Author, 'The Innovation Manager's Desk Reference'

"WARNING: This book will radically transform your thinking."

– Matt R Johnson, Director, Cyber Security for a major global financial institution, UK

"Inspirational, thought provoking, full of energy.... Dream BIG.
Jen Fraser shows you how."

– Ted Delanghe, Author, 'Ideas Risks and Magic'

"You can tell the doctors and surgeons who've read 'Everyone's a
Genius' from those who haven't - their curiosity and love of science has
been rekindled, and they now remember **why** they decided to practice
medicine in the first place. This can only be good for patient outcomes."

– A. Cullinan, Clinical Systems Trainer for a Sydney Hospital, Australia.

"Jen Fraser has written a positive, lively and readable book which
should encourage the reader to 'think outside the box'."

– John Adair, Author, 'The Art of Creative Thinking'

"Thoroughly interesting read that actively challenged my perception
of what it means to be innovative. Jen Fraser takes you through a
logical progression of ideas and concepts - many backed up with
evidence - which will enlighten, build or validate depending upon
your own experience."

*– Jamie Baggaley, Principal Consultant, Customer Communication
Management, Fuji Xerox, Australia*

"Loved your book. I hope it does well because **humanity needs it.**"

– Robin Landry, Singer Songwriter, USA

"This is self-help for sceptics. Jen Fraser points out ingenuity-killers in our common cultural assumptions, and offers substitutes from science, science fiction, business, and a host of history's most influential thinkers.

In explaining ideation, Jen Fraser adopts the familiar forms of the self-help book, but instead of the usual tosh she fills it with common-sense guidance. Without a doubt her soundest prescription is to surround yourself with a club of people to exchange, critique and refine ideas. Fancy people call this an 'active learning set', but Fraser is more basic and tells us to create our 'own little Renaissance'. She writes in plain Australian English and illustrates her words with beautiful pen-and-ink sketches. It's rather like a well-designed platter of exquisite dips: her paragraphs and chapters are impactful and well-organised, designed for a reader to take a little bit at a time."

– Lynette Nusbacher, MA DPhil, Devil's Advocate,
Nusbacher Associates, London, UK

"Bookstores are crowded with too many books on creativity and innovation. Most are wordy door stops filled with too many words and too little inspiring or useful content.

CLEAR THE SHELVES! Make room for Jen Fraser's beaming, brilliant *'Everyone's a Genius'*. Nearly every page is alive with playful, profound, and practical challenges and delight-filled illustrations to encourage *anyone* to explore their passions—discovering full potential. Can't imagine you are a genius? Jen Fraser has big, plans for you."

– C. McNair Wilson, Former Disney Imagineer
and author of 'HATCH!'

CopyCat: How to Escape
Status Quo Thinking
& Lead the Field

everyone's a
GENIUS

Simple Tips to Boost
Your Brilliance *Now*

Written & illustrated by

JEN FRASER

Foreword by

PIERS ANTHONY

CONTENT 100% CREATED BY HUMAN INTELLIGENCE

An Ideation Training Book
First published 2014, by Ideation Training Pty Ltd, Ipswich Qld Australia.
This corrected reprint edition published 2025.

Ordering Information:

Special discounts are available on quantity purchases by corporations, associations, educational institutions, and others. For details, visit outthinx.com or email hello@outthinx.com.

National Library of Australia Cataloguing-in-Publication entry:
Fraser, Jennifer Lynn, 1975— author, illustrator.
Everyone's a genius : simple tips to boost your brilliance now /
written & illustrated by Jen Fraser; foreword by Piers Anthony Jacob.
Includes bibliographical references and index.
Anthony Jacob, Piers, 1934— writer of added text.
180 p. 20 cm.

ISBN 978-0-9941715-0-4 (hardback)   ISBN 978-0-9941715-2-8 (ebook: ePub)
ISBN 978-0-9941715-1-1 (paperback)   ISBN 978-0-9941715-3-5 (ebook: Kindle)
ISBN 978-0-9941715-4-2 (audiobook)

1.Innovation mindset; 2.Creative ability in business; 3.Creative thinking;
4.Self-realization; 5.New business enterprises; 6.Success in business.

Dewey Number: 153.35

Email: hello@jen-fraser.com
Website: **jen-fraser.com**

Contents

Foreword

by Piers Anthony

I read *Everyone's A Genius* by Jen Fraser, who also illustrated it with nice pictures. I'm impressed with their clarity, having once aspired to be an artist myself. This foreword leads me into an extended discussion that is more about me than the book, perhaps a familiar story to those who read my columns.

The book starts with a quote attributed to Albert Einstein to the effect that if you judge a fish by its ability to climb a tree, it will think it is stupid.

That registers with me, as all my life I have been bothered by false comparisons, such as devising an IQ test tuned to the lifestyle of upper-class whites so that blacks score 15 points lower, supposed evidence of their inferiority.

I've always been somewhat of a square peg, so that I scored low on tests until I caught on and learned to cater to their notions of correctness, and then my IQ rose from the cellar to the top one or two percent.

Sure, they say intelligence doesn't change, but I say measured IQ does because of the fallibility of the tests, and I got a brainful of that; don't get me started.

I have been called a genius by some readers, though I haven't been certain of their definition of the term; my guess is that they mean they really like my writing. So I approached this book with interest, hoping it would clarify such matters, and wasn't disappointed.

This is, to a degree, a self-help book, positive attitude, smile and the world smiles with you exhortation. Yes, be positive, but hew close to realism too.

This book recommends going for the different idea, the one others dismiss out of hand, but does acknowledge that the vast majority of new ideas may be erroneous.

I think of that as like evolution: 99% of mutations may be bad, but the 1% that are good are responsible for making us what we are today. So condemning the 99% may be a losing strategy, since you don't know which wild notion is the 1%. You need to give serious unbiased attention to them all, to winnow out that one.

There's a fair amount of discussion of genius here, and I like it.

"A genius uses creative and radically different thinking where everything we believe we 'know' is up for debate."

Maybe by that definition I might indeed lay some claim to genius.

Farther along it says that some geniuses don't have high IQs. That Albert Einstein's IQ was never tested, and that he flunked some exams. That there are great entrepreneurs without degrees, such as the founders of Virgin Airlines, Ford Motors, Dell Computers, KFC, McDonalds, Apple, Coca-Cola, Disney, the inventor Tesla, and Bill Gates of Microsoft.

I'm betting that they all felt stifled by conventional education, and rebelled against it. But it should be noted that for every such success, there are a myriad failures.

A study conducted over four weeks shows that writing down your goals increases you chances of achieving them by an extra 50%. Better still, if you tell a friend your goals every week, this rate increases to 77%.

Hmmm. So what about me? Did I write down a clear plan to become a successful novelist?

Actually I did, pretty much, because I had to go for my BA in Creative Writing. I did wind up vastly more successful than classmates, though it took more than a decade, but somehow I doubt that's the reason. At times it felt like navigating my canoe through a hurricane at sea as I encountered those who had no intention of being decent or fair and sought to wash me out for standing on my rights and telling the truth. You buck the system at your own high risk. It takes more than a dream to survive that.

The book recommends becoming a dreamer who takes action, rather than simply dreaming.

I did that, in spades.

My goal was like a shining beacon, and I never lost sight of it. But there was a hell of a lot more to it than just the dream, as these asides hint. Something I've noted is that the top performers in any discipline tend to have their lives taken over by it, and it is that total dedication, coupled with talent and chance, that makes the difference.

It was true for me. I had one exception from the outset: I never let my career interfere with my family.

Oh, it tried, in my heyday as a bestseller; my wife became known as Mrs. Piers Anthony (it's a pseudonym), and my daughters when they went to college swore their friends to secrecy so they would not be known as my children.

It's hard to wall fame out.

But if at any point I had had to choose between my career and my family, I would have dumped the career, albeit it with phenomenal regret. There's the key.

Fortunately my wife supported me absolutely, through some perilous passes, and that's a significant part of my success. It's been 58 years now, and death will us part. Is there genius for lasting marriage?

The book stresses the importance of getting on with your dream instead of sitting on your duff. Then stay with it until you see it through. Finish what you start. Understand your limitations and work within them, not against yourself. All good advice.

Then it tackles **major myths**.

Don't buy into the myth that being smart will make you happy. The author cites the example of her friend who joined Mensa, the club for smart folk, and found that very few members were interested in creating or inventing anything; instead they were focused on solving puzzles and games.

That was my impression.

Long ago I considered taking the Mensa test, which I surely could have passed — my mother was a member — but was not impressed with their agenda, and passed it by. I love puzzles and games, but I love writing more.

That creative thinking is linked to IQ: tests show that the two have little to do with each other.

That's my impression too.

I regard myself as one of the most creative folk extant, with a breadth of imagination like no other, but that is not at all the same as IQ or even writing ability.

What about the arts of composing, dancing, painting, or poetry, which are not measured by IQ? They are the essence of creativity, as is original story telling.

That geniuses are brilliant at everything. No, outside their fields they are duffers like the rest of us. That ordinary folk are not creative. No, we are born creative, could we just hang on to our potential. That you need fancy equipment to be great. You don't, though it can help.

And so on.

The book also objects to closed minds; curious minds are better. But here I have a caveat: it says to change "That's impossible" to "How can this be made possible?" Some things are impossible; I know, as I earn my living from writing fantasy, the literature of the impossible.

We're not going to build a spaceship that exceeds the speed of light. Oh, yes, we can ponder wormholes in space, thus bypassing that limitation, but this is a devious process even in conjecture.

We're not going to travel backward in time; alternate universes may be our best way around that, again devious in application. We're not going to resolve paradoxes; "This statement is false" is not subject to refutation.

But I do prefer open minds, and abhor the damage done by closed minds in authority. It's best to be exceedingly careful about what we declare to be impossible.

Overall, this book is an appeal for open mindedness, and I applaud it, and recommend it to anyone who feels stifled by ordinary existence. Or, as it says, feeling like a rat in a cage.

One huge example is education; we are locked into an archaic pattern that tends to stifle imagination and progress; I know, having survived it as a student, then as a teacher.

How could this be changed?

The book points out that Finland is an outstanding example. In the 1960s they decided on reform, and in one generation they went from mediocre to superior. There, teaching is high status and testing is minimal; school shopping is unknown because all their schools are good. The rest of the world could profit enormously by emulating their example.

Another is the Pareto Principle, that states that about 80% of effects come from 20% of causes.

This applies in business and in crime (the two are not necessarily synonymous), and working with it can significantly increase a person's effectiveness.

And I am mentioned, for my novel *Dragon on a Pedestal*, with little Ivy's magic ability to Enhance salient qualities of those she encounters; thus taming the most fearsome dragon in Xanth.

Not that I noticed the reference, of course.

Piers Anthony
New York Times Best Selling Author
www.HiPiers.com

everyone's a
GENIUS

Introduction

Ideation is the spring from which all innovation flows.

This book is about idea generation (ideation), on radically original thinking. If used correctly, it will help you come up with a vastly better quality of idea than ever before.

Truly brilliant ideas often arrive unexpectedly, seemingly out of the blue and at the most random and inconvenient of times. You can bring about these "eureka" moments more often and more reliably simply by using the many proven and repeatable methods I have gathered together for you.

So read on dear friend, and hold on tight as we take a trip on the great adventure that is ideation.....

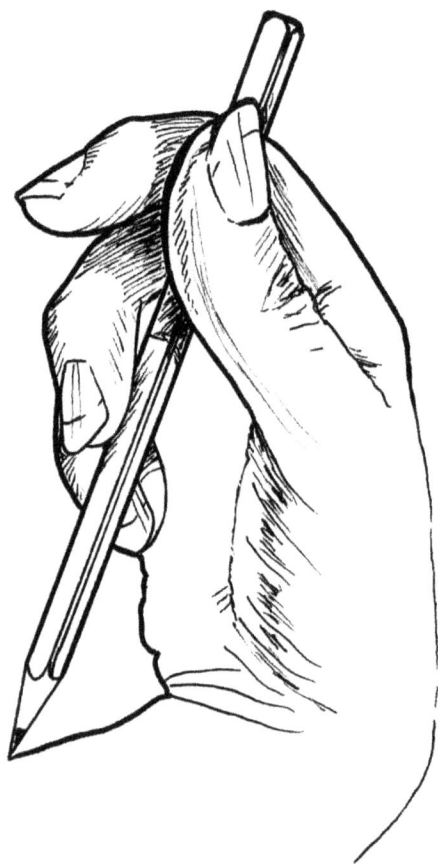

1. Choose Success

IF I CAN DO IT, YOU CAN TOO

A few years ago I made several of the techniques in this book a regular day-to-day part of my life. My efforts were rewarded by personally coming up with a major scientific, award-winning idea.

Sadly for me, I was about 30 years too late! The idea had already been discovered, tested and accepted as theory. On the bright side, I had proven to myself that many of the techniques I share with you in this book have genuinely worked, do work, and can work for you.

If you're curious to know more, I reveal how I came up with this especially brilliant idea at the end of this book.

At left, my hand seems to be drawing itself into existence, just as ideas would appear to come from nowhere. Idea generation and drawing both require patience, persistence and concentration. With a bit of practise, such skills get easier as you go and yield better results.

But first, let's take a quick look at a few words which have, from time to time, suffered from a case of mistaken identity:

INVENTION, INNOVATION OR IDEATION?

If necessity is the mother; ideation is the father of invention.

'Necessity' is when you have a problem you need to solve.

For example, the windshield wiper invented by Mary Anderson in 1903 was the first workable solution for driving safely in the rain.

Since then, many designers have made improvements to it, but on the whole these have been tweaks and alterations (innovations), rather than a completely different approach altogether (an invention).

In contrast to innovation, **radically original thinking** (ideation) can produce totally new answers to tackle big-picture or abstract problems. Problems which perhaps no-one else has thought of as being a problem, until they see the solution and think "ah, but of course - pure genius!"

- New *innovations* are often developed following the statement **"I wish..."** (it would do something it doesn't already do).
- New *inventions* come about with **"How can I...?"** (solve the problem).
- Blue sky thinking and *ideation* begin with **"What if...?"** (we're totally wrong about our assumptions. What if we really can do XYZ?).

During an ideation session, a person or team focuses on coming up with lots of new ideas: to invent, to innovate, or both.

This book contains simple methods to change the way you think; to help you view the world through the eyes of a genius ideator.

"While you're already thinking, why not think really BIG?"
– American saying

GENIUS OR TALENTED?

A genius uses creative and radically different thinking, where everything we believe we 'know' is up for debate. The terrific news is that coming up with a 'genius' idea can be achieved in a very short space of time, by anyone willing to learn how to think differently.

In comparison, talent doesn't mean having to be creative or even original. The current thinking around talent is that it takes 7-10 years of constantly honing your particular skill before you might be considered talented. It takes a huge amount of dedication and hard work.

> "I put all my genius into my life;
> I put only my talent into my works."
> – *Oscar Wilde*

The obvious exception to this rule is the child prodigy.

A paper published in the journal Intelligence in 2012 found a common link between the seven child prodigies in their study: they all excelled in working memory performance. This is the ability to hang on to a thought when interrupted, or to juggle lots of on-going activities at the same time. They are masters of multitasking.

It's a bit late for you and me (to be child prodigies) but it's never too late to work on improving useful skills. Skills such as ideation.

For much of this first chapter on **choice** and **setting goals**, we'll take a half step back, and start thinking about the biggest influences on your everyday decision making. You'll have a good think about where you've been, before making any decisions about where you're going.

WHERE ARE YOU GOING?

Q: What were YOU put on this Earth to do before you die?

Don't know? That's OK. In this chapter we'll look at ways to help you discover your future direction, then get you going on that path.

For those of you who do already have an answer to the question above, we'll look at discovering the root causes - the real reasons - behind why you're not already living your life as you wish. We'll look at ways to find out what's been holding you back, and start you off in a nice straight line toward your big goal.

Either way, you must first ask yourself: "How did I come to be where I am today?"

Maybe you've suffered terrible hardships, which you feel have been holding you back. Or maybe your life has trundled on without thought for where it will lead. Whatever your situation, to change your future direction you must change the one making the decisions: **you**.

If only changing our habits was easy. If it was, you wouldn't see rows and rows of shelves groaning with weight loss books and diet plans in stores around the world. Sure, you can make a choice, but sticking with that choice for the long haul - that's where most people just give up.

> "Life is like a grindstone -
> it will either grind you down or sharpen you up.
> Whichever happens is your decision."
> *– adapted from Thomas Holdcroft*

RUNNING ON AUTO-PILOT

Do you realise how ingrained your everyday habits really are? Every little daily task you have is practically a ritual, one you don't spend any time thinking about. The next time you go to brush your teeth, try using the opposite hand. You'll be amazed at how much focus and attention it takes you to complete a simple everyday task - one which you perform like a ritual the same way each day.

The lesson here is: it is much easier to keep doing things the same way you've always done them, than to **suffer the discomfort of trying out something new**. It is my hope that you become much more aware of how much of your life is actually run on auto-pilot.

> "To learn - one effort;
> to unlearn - two."
> – *Montenegrin Proverb*

When you try to break a habit, you need lots of dedication and focus to make it stay broken. Instead, why not try to **dissolve** a habit, by gradually replacing it with the shiny new habit you actually want.

My neighbour helped people to quit smoking by telling them to hold a drinking straw, a pen, or a rosary - something to **get used to** fiddling with instead of a cigarette. By discovering what their existing habits were, it was simple to build up shiny new habits to replace them.

Healthier habits can extend your life, so make a start on dissolving away bad habits. Let's move on now - let's look at the past to see how it affects your decisions today, and how you choose your future direction.

MOVE FORWARD

And what about your past? Do not think you are alone in having suffered life's hardships. You don't know everyone else's story.

A group of businessmen stopped in for dinner at a hotel in outback Queensland, miles from anywhere. Their waitress spoke 'none too good' and with a heavy drawl. One of these businessmen assumed she was only the restaurant owner's daughter and proceeded to give her a hard time. His friend asked how she came to be working there, and her story amazed them all.

She was from the most deprived, crime-ridden, and drug-dependent suburb in Melbourne, about 2,000kms away, or 21 hours nonstop by car. Since she couldn't get a job there, she searched the whole continent for work, any work, leaving her boyfriend behind, to be here in a small rural town with more cattle than people.

Rather than sit back and accept a future of poverty she took drastic action, even if it meant being miles away from her network of friends and family to call on for support.

Having heard her story, the businessmen were embarrassed by their assumptions and treated her with more respect.

Never forget others are having a much tougher time of it than you, but are moving forward just the same.

Why not follow their example?

"Reflect upon your blessings, of which everyone has plenty, not on your past misfortunes, of which all men have some."
– Charles Dickens

KILL EXCUSES, HAVE REASONS

Even inaction is a decision. No-one would have blamed the young waitress for staying home where her family and friends were. No-one would be surprised if she'd turned to a life of crime and drugs - it's what's expected in the area she grew up.

To be successful in life you must not let anything stand in your way. Especially excuses. Thankfully, you can apply several of the ideation tips from this book to come up with solutions for having greater control of your future. The first thing you need to do however is to be **honest** with yourself. Look closely at what's been holding you back - are they only excuses or genuinely valid reasons?

> "You should not be satisfied being a victim, nor with being a survivor. You should aim to be a conqueror."
>
> *– Dr Laura Schlessinger*

If you were mistreated as a child and believe there is nothing for you but to be miserable forever - this is a life lived behind an excuse. It's an excuse because you know you can do something about it - you can take steps to move on, to become whole again. Instead of an excuse, a valid reason would be: I'm getting help to deal with my past, and I'm looking forward to the day I've truly dealt with it, when it stops having such a huge impact on my life.

That's not letting anything stand in your way. That's a case of getting on with becoming the person you want to be. That's your choice, it's up to you.

Hopefully this next story will inspire you to focus on what you can do, rather than what you can't.

Imagine for a moment that what began as a sore throat actually led to having all four of your limbs amputated.

This is exactly what happened to Australian Matthew Ames in June 2012, who survived streptococcal toxic shock. Rather than wallow in the devastating loss of his independence, he chose to focus, not on what he **can't** do, but on what he **can** do.

When he is not working hard on rehabilitation Matthew shares his story to inspire others. He has a real sparkle in his eyes and an incredible passion for life. Matthew's is a life filled with love from his wife, his four energetic young children and the support of his extended family and many friends.

Matthew's hope for the future is the replacement of all four of his limbs. He is already making progress, being able to stand up on his own, using 'interim' feet. To read more about his courageous journey visit: *www.renovatingmatthew.com*

HEAD VERSUS HEART

Many motivational speakers tell their audience to only improve their strengths, and ignore their weaknesses. But to truly move forward, the weaknesses which lead you to make poor decisions time and time again, really need to be addressed.

In controlling yourself, you control your future.

Why do some folk spend all their money, the very moment it comes in? Have you ever wondered why a friend is deeper in debt than ever before, so soon after a big pay rise? Or why some ladies keep on dating the same type of men, hoping in vain, to find Mr Right?

In the case of money, sometimes it's a childish attitude ("I want...") or a lack of patience ("I want it now") that causes a person the most trouble; rather than a failure to understand money management. They can choose to do nothing, to stay on the current course of action - but at what cost? The missed opportunities, the time lost when the problem is finally addressed twenty years down the track, when it could have been fixed today. It really is best to fix a problem sooner than later.

In the case of finding Mr Right, I've advised friends to date someone they're not at first attracted to - someone who is not their 'type' and to just see where it leads. What can it hurt? If it doesn't work out, hey you didn't expect it to anyway, right? This advice has led to happy marriages for several of my friends, rather than the unhappy cycle they were previously stuck in.

> "If you do the same thing you've always done,
> you'll get the same results you always get."
> – *attributed to Albert Einstein*

TOUGH LOVE

Sometimes what initially seems like a disaster can be turned into a fantastic opportunity - if you choose to see it as such. The British might call this 'character building' or stoicism. Most tales of survival from the Australian outback feature a spirit of sheer bloody-minded determination. Like walking for 5 days straight on a broken ankle until finally reaching civilisation. This mental toughness has no time for excuses: it's do or die. It comes as no surprise that Aussies are known for dishing out advice in the form of **tough love**. It goes a bit like this:

Bruce: "I wish someone would give me a job, but I don't have a zillion years worth of experience."

Kylie: "What a load of rubbish. Get off your backside and go do something about it. Stop hiding behind excuses."

Bruce: "I thought you were my friend."

Kylie: "I *am* your friend - that's why I'm doing you a favour and telling you to quit your whining. Go knock on every door or something. Just don't sit around here wishing your life away."

Bruce: "I hate you."

Kylie: "But I'm right, go on, admit it."

Bruce: "Never." ***sigh***

The belief around giving tough love advice is that; if you really care about someone you'll deliver some brutally honest advice (not pulling any punches) in the hope it will jolt them into taking action. It's like teaching a young bird to fly by pushing it out of the nest.

Sure, there are much *gentler* ways to teach the bird, but none so quick and effective.

Philosopher Friedrich Nietzsche was famous for his saying "what doesn't kill you makes you stronger." He believed it's only through adversity that we can realise our greatest achievements. He wished misfortune and bad luck for all his closest friends with the hope they would *overcome adversity* and realise their full potential.

"To those human beings who are of any concern to me,
I wish suffering, desolation, sickness, ill-treatment,
indignities, profound self contempt, the torture of self
mistrust and the wretchedness of the vanquished."

– Friedrich Nietzsche

SUCCESS

Wanting to *'show 'em what you're made of'* can be a fantastic motivator. A great example in recent years is the headline story of Andreas Panayiotou, a London-based real estate tycoon reportedly worth £400 million, who personally built his wealth - despite being unable to read.

He broke the news of his 'secret shame' to the press during the Evening Standard's *'Get London Reading'* campaign in 2011. He was able to hide his illiteracy for two decades because of his fantastic memory and the help of his personal assistant.

Setting aside all excuses and working toward making their dreams a reality, entrepreneurs often hire highly qualified staff to come work for them. Why climb someone else's ladder when you can just own the ladder yourself? Success really is the best revenge.

Great entrepreneurs without degrees include:

Sir Richard Branson (Virgin), Ingvar Kamprad (IKEA), Henry Ford (Ford Cars), Michael Dell (Dell Computers), Colonel Sanders (KFC), Ray Kroc (McDonalds), Steve Wozniak (Apple), Charles Culpeper (Coca Cola) and Walt Disney. The great inventor Nikola Tesla also dropped out of university, and Bill Gates is Harvard's most successful dropout.

Of course, you don't need to drop-out, in order to build a world-spanning empire! This list just proves that success in business has nothing to do with your grades in school, college or university.

That's one less excuse to hold you back.

NO TURNING BACK

A terrifyingly effective way to become 100% determined to achieve your goal is to cut off your exit.

I recall the ancient tale of an Asian general who sailed his fleet overnight to his enemy's shores. While the army slept, he ordered their own ships burned into the sea. When they awoke, he said there was no going back - they must win or perish.

They won.

When there is no exit plan, you can be sure you'll absolutely give it everything you've got!

I love the story of New Zealand-born physicist Ernest Rutherford, who, among other things, was the first person to split the atom. In the early years of his research, he is reported to have addressed his colleagues in the lab with:

"Gentlemen, we haven't any money, so now we must think."

In the years following this statement, Rutherford and four of his students made many great discoveries which led each of them to being awarded a Nobel Prize.

Whether we realise it or not, every one of us is already on a one-way trip with no exit clause. And that trip is towards death:

A LIFE WITH FEW REGRETS

There's a new trend popping up in sleepy neighbourhoods all over the world. They're called Death Cafés, and they are places where the taboo subject is openly discussed and pondered.

Regular reminders of death (*memento mori*) can help you filter out the fluff and noise of daily life, to focus on the things which really matter to you. Reminders of death have driven and motivated countless great and successful people throughout history.

> "The people most afraid to die are the ones
> who know they have never really lived."
>
> *– Henry David Thoreau*

You can gain or lose money; but time... time you can only lose.

For the decisions you make today, imagine looking back over your life as a 100 year old. What kind of person will you have grown into? Will you have achieved what you set out to do?

How many regrets will you have and which decisions will haunt you the most?

At the end of your life, the only one you need to have pleased is the face staring back at you in the mirror.

On my final day of high school, a teacher wrote down a short poem from memory, into my yearbook.

It stands out because it is the only depressing thing written in it. I remember being confused at the time.

Of all the things she could have chosen to write, why this?

DREAMS

The poem was titled *'Dreams'* and was written by American poet and activist Langston Hughes. His beautiful poem can be found in countless English textbooks around the world.

This concise eight line poem warns us all against wasting the precious short time we have.

I recommend you take the time to find it, read it, and reflect on this illustration when you do.

WHAT YOU CAN DO

Still not coping with a traumatic past? Take action: get professional help so you can heal and have a better future. The best way to view a low point in your life is to believe that things can only get better.

Give up on identifying yourself as any sort of victim. Understand your own strengths and know you are genuinely a worthwhile person.

Stop simply surviving and be a conqueror instead: confront your own doubts and fears so the bullies of this world will never have sway over you ever again.

Stop comparing your achievements or cleverness with others. You only ever compete with, test and challenge **yourself** on your life journey, not others. You never know how great you can be, until you take action and really try it out for yourself.

When faced with a disastrous situation, consider that it might be a great opportunity in disguise. For example, the aftermath of a natural disaster could be a good time to build new friendships or to start living your life in a new way. There are opportunities all around us every day, you just need to look for them.

Do not listen to the dream stealers. How would they know what you are really capable of? They have their own secret list of regrets, wishing they'd been bold enough to take action in their youth.

2. "The Road to Paradise is... Paradise."

– old Spanish proverb

Life is a journey. And on that journey, it's important to stop, think, and appreciate what you have now, before these days are long gone. Simply trying out new things and generating brand new ideas can be a fulfilling means to its own end.

When musicians first start out they have complete artistic freedom. They can experiment until they 'find' their own unique sound. Once a band is famous, their loyal fans either walk out or riot if they try performing an experimental new sound on stage. The fans want what they paid for: more of that same old, familiar sound.

Attached to one of the staff room doors at the Queensland College of Art where I studied for three years, was a sign saying:

"The road to paradise is... paradise."

For many musicians, artists and writers, the ***journey*** towards stardom was the most personally fulfilling, most exciting time of their lives. To recapture that feeling they'd need to start a whole new journey into the unknown, with all the risks and excitement that go with it.

When you're setting out on a new journey, looking to achieve a new life goal; be sure to choose something for the sheer love of it, not just for the money so that it can be its own reward. Birthing this awesome new product, masterpiece or idea into the world is an incredible experience.

So stay with it for the long haul: reputation and success are built up over time. ***It's a marathon not a sprint.***

END GAME

Sit down, relax, and take some time to ponder this: Imagine you are a billionaire and have achieved your big life goals.

OK so what now? You've bought all the luxury cars and property you ever wanted to own plus more. You've also retired early and travelled the world, and now are wondering what to do with yourself. What now? Will you dedicate the rest of your life to charity work? Or will you focus on family, build a new business, invest in real estate, or perhaps even support budding entrepreneurs?

Once you have brushed aside any hunger you might have for expensive experiences, you can drill down and discover what you ***really*** want out of life.

It finally becomes crystal clear what your true interests are.

"Of the billionaires I have known, money just brings out the basic traits in them. If they were jerks before they had money, they are simply jerks with a billion dollars."

– *Warren Buffet*

PLAN YOUR BRIDGE

> "A goal is a dream
> with a deadline."
> – *Napoleon Hill*

Build a bridge between today and your future.

Plan a series of little steps in the direction of your goal, and cross off your progress as you go. Be sure to celebrate each milestone as you reach it. This will do wonders to keep you on-track and motivated, as long as your end goal is something you're passionate about.

It's so much better than looking at your end goal across the waters and thinking to yourself "it's all too much, I'll never get there."

As the saying goes; How do you eat an elephant?

One bite at a time.

WHAT AM I GOOD AT?

CAN'T SHUT YOU UP. When you chat with friends, do you steer the conversation back around to the same topic? It's what you're already interested in - this is one of your passions.

EXPLORE. Set aside half an hour every day to browse through different magazines, Wikipedia or other fascinating sources to discover what does or does not interest you.

JOIN. There are loads of social clubs and online communities with folk just as passionate on your subject as you are.

BE STRONG. Don't blindly follow trends and mainstream beliefs, think for yourself. Don't worry if your passion is for something weird or unpopular. You might just find yourself setting trends in the future.

TWO CHOICES. Stuck between two equally good possibilities? Flip a coin. Before you even look at the coin, you'll often know which side you're really hoping for - or which would disappoint you the most. You don't need to stick with the decision from the flipped coin, just make up your own mind.

TEST IT OUT. Find someone already in a job you're thinking of doing and arrange to shadow them while they work. If they're too busy, offer to buy them coffee to find out what they think of their job. *If you don't ask, you don't get.*

POLL. Speak with your closest friends and family who know you better than you do, and ask them "what are my strengths?" Not just for abilities but character traits too. Consider their answers, and think about what your future would look like if you worked at improving these strengths, or minimising your weaknesses.

KEEP A HOBBY

Unfortunately, just being good at something or loving an activity doesn't always mean you should turn it into your day job, or build a new business around it.

> "When you marry your mistress,
> you create a job vacancy."
> – *Sir James Goldsmith*

What's to stop a man divorcing and marrying his mistress, when it's something he's done before? The danger he faces is in getting stuck in an endless cycle of dissatisfaction and upheaval.

The same goes for leaving your job to take up a hobby full time. It seemed like such a good idea at first. What began as fun and exciting, ended up being more exhausting than the job you left. At least back then you had paid sick leave and normal hours. Now you're working long days and weekends.

Where did it all go wrong?

When self employed, stick to working regular hours. It focuses your efforts because tasks need to be done quickly when you no longer believe you have got all day, night and weekends to fall back on. Burn-out is disastrous for your health and happiness, so exercise some self-discipline and separate work time from leisure time.

What will you do with all that precious spare time now?

With your hobby as your job, you'll need to take up another new hobby or two. Only this time, don't go turning it into a job as well.

HOW TO GET LUCKY

How much does luck factor into success?

Can a person take action to become more lucky?

In his book *'The Luck Factor'* Dr Richard Wiseman reveals the results of a rigorous scientific study on luck.

He found that blind chance favours nobody - lucky or unlucky. The participants who believed themselves 'lucky' were in fact creating their own luck through attitude.

They possessed a highly accurate intuition, thereby trusting in their gut instincts. They had a 'no excuses' attitude, higher levels of perseverance, and greater courage when pursuing opportunities. As optimists they simply bought more tickets and entered more competitions than others, which in turn increased their chances for success.

Their high expectations of future wealth and happiness often became self-fulfilling prophecies.

So the great news is that anybody can actually become luckier just by changing their attitude.

But let's not be so irresponsible as to leave our fates to chance! That's just asking for trouble, as you'll see on the next page.

There are actions we can all take to increase our chances for success, and it all begins with making written plans and pledging ourselves to them.

WRITE IT DOWN

> "If you fail to plan, you plan to fail."
> – *Benjamin Franklin, attributed*

Are your personal goals written down? Do you refer back to these every week? Daily?

Have you heard the tale about how 3% of Yale or Harvard students with written goals make over ten times more money than the other 97% (with unwritten goals) put together? This urban myth is so popular you can read about it on thousands of websites today.

Fortunately, Dr Gail Matthews, a professor at the Dominican University in California, ran a four week study on written goals with 267 participants across six countries, from various backgrounds.

Her findings revealed that the participants with written goals were over 50% more likely to achieve them than those without written goals. On top of this, if you tell your goals to a friend every week, the rate jumps to a 77% improvement to successful achievement of goals.

Good habits and accountability win the race.

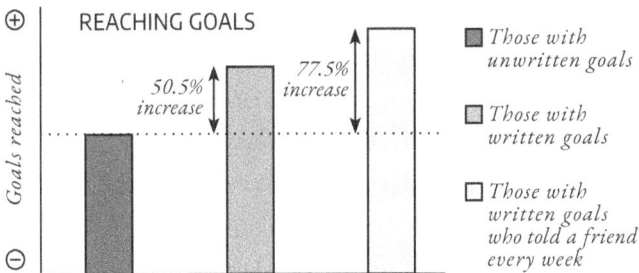

REACHING GOALS

⊕ Goals reached ⊖

50.5% increase

77.5% increase

■ Those with unwritten goals

■ Those with written goals

□ Those with written goals who told a friend every week

TAKE ACTION

Success = seeking opportunities + preparedness + ACTION.

Become a dreamer who takes action, not one who simply dreams. Whatever it is you want to do with your life - do some research, make plans, shortlist from your ideation session on what would be the ***best way*** to achieve your plan, then take action.

Build a bridge between today and your future, then walk that bridge.

But how do you know when to give up on a plan?

Only you can know how much you can take before you break, but by far the ***greatest threat*** to success is in giving up too soon.

> "When I thought I couldn't go on,
> I forced myself to keep going.
> My success is based on persistence, not luck."
>
> *– Estee Lauder*

IF AT FIRST YOU DON'T SUCCEED

Try a different way. How many times can you handle rejection before giving up? Five? Twenty?

How about 1,000 times?

If you'd like to hear the ultimate story of sheer bloody-minded determination, look no further than the incredible story of Colonel Sanders, who was 65 years old when he started KFC.

While most others his age were already enjoying their retirement, Colonel Sanders took action with extreme persistence in the face of on-going rejection, and ended up building an empire like nothing else.

These three charts show levels of success as time moves on, for when you *a)* don't take action, *b)* don't have a plan, or *c)* follow your plan. As you can see, a dream dies very quickly when no action is taken; without a plan the path can be torturous and chaotic; and when you stick with a plan success can skyrocket suddenly, albeit with a few hurdles and setbacks along the way.

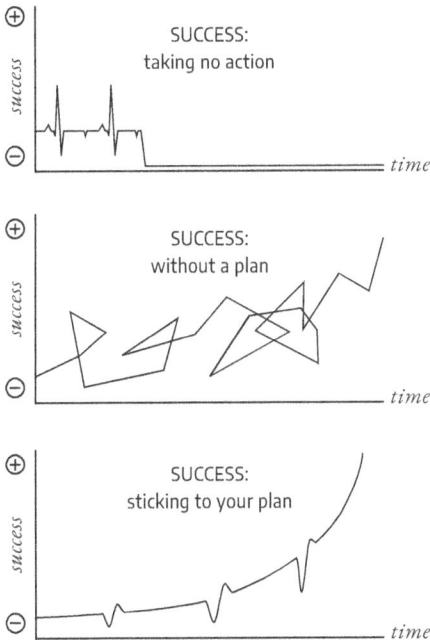

SUCCESS:
taking no action

SUCCESS:
without a plan

SUCCESS:
sticking to your plan

Once you've finally made your decision, you've planned out all the little steps you need to take in order to reach your great goal, there is one more little problem to be dealt with, an issue that will crop up all the way along your journey....

GOOD-BYE PROCRASTINATION

Q: Why do people procrastinate?

A: To avoid that uncomfortable feeling, that unease, that goes hand in hand with doing something for the first time. Forming a new habit isn't always easy, but finding something else to do sure is.

To avoid the pain of that clumsy or 'out of your depth' feeling, you end up doing all sorts of things instead like housework, gardening, playing games or watching TV. You name it - whatever can be done, is done, to put off what you know you 'should' be working on.

> "Know the true value of time; snatch, seize,
> and enjoy every moment of it.
> No idleness; no laziness; no procrastination;
> never put off until tomorrow what you can do today."
> – *Lord Chesterfield*

Just consider this one fact.

Those small tasks which you've done countless times before are comforting. They're less frightening than doing something new. Carrying out known tasks while avoiding an unfamiliar one is the most common sign of procrastination.

But how to tackle procrastination? The answer is to look at your reasons and your excuses. Look at what it is about the task that makes you feel uncomfortable. Once you've found the root cause of a problem you can work on solving it. Look at all the excuses which are helping you procrastinate, and ideate up a range of ways you might go about addressing them - including also asking others for their thoughts and ideas.

Sometimes you put off a task to give yourself a few more days to mull over the problem or sleep on it. Or maybe you work best under the stress and excitement of a short deadline. If so, try setting yourself an artificially early deadline, one that's more convenient for your diary and helps you enjoy guilt-free leisure time later on.

Try using the carrot approach. Tell a friend you'll enjoy a special reward only when the task is done - they can help you stay on target. Don't beat yourself up if your task takes longer to finish than you thought. Keep making good steady progress rather than throw in the towel.

Make sure you get Unfinished Objects (UFOs) out of your life now and keep 'em out. How many UFOs do you have languishing in your home? Give them away, throw them out, or if you must, stick to a schedule and actually finish them. They're terrible little agents for procrastination, when you're meant to be doing something much more important.

Say good-bye to procrastination by ideating up a range of ways to keep things moving, coupled with a spot of self discipline.

You might also try imagining for a moment that you will never die. With all the time in the world to get around to finishing your projects, why bother doing any of them right now? Just sit back, relax, and enjoy today with no care for the future. Yuck! It's just as well we're mortal, because with limitless time nothing would ever get done.

So do it today because tomorrow might have other plans for you.

What you put off today haunts your tomorrows.

ROOT CAUSE

If I had let procrastination get the better of me, you would not be reading this book right now.

I had everything lined up, ready to get busy writing. I'd already decided on the chapter headings and bullet points, but still my head was swimming with excuses and I couldn't get settled. So I did what any good ideator would do and slept on it. I finally realised my problem was a love of being succinct and to the point. Fleshing out my gazillions of bullet points into paragraphs is what was really bothering me.

Having discovered my true objection, I now realised all my other reasons were nothing more than silly excuses.

Having **identified** the problem, now it was time to ideate possible solutions to **remove all obstacles** to my progress.

I vowed to work on my laptop at the local library, where the air-conditioning would be quiet and free (solving my "it's too hot to work" objection), and I would be away from the easy distractions of the internet and TV.

Just before heading out the door I decided to try writing at home once more, and wouldn't you just know it, the writer's block completely vanished. I was off and typing. As an aside, yes I did indeed write part of this book at the Queensland State Library.

Another boost to my frame of mind came from swapping my comfy house clothes for nice ones more suited to off-site work. Something which had not been obvious to me until that moment.

I gave myself one more liberty, which was to write any chapter I felt like, instead of just starting at the beginning. After all, it's much better to get some work done than none at all.

A creative mind can sometimes jump around all over the place and I have learned to follow my creative juices where they lead me (when I have the luxury of time to do so). I trust that my unconscious mind knows what it's doing, since it is much **cleverer than I am**.

Just getting started is usually the hardest part of any new project. Seeing it through to the end is the next.

STAYING THE DISTANCE

Always finish what you start. The first step on the road to success is in recognising you're not superhuman - you've only so much time and energy to devote to any one thing at a time.

Understand your own limitations and work within them, not against yourself.

Promise yourself to work only on projects where you will be devoted enough and consistent enough, to see them right through to the end. Tick off a list of small steps toward building your bridge, and work on those parts which interest you the most. Then see how far you've come, how near the end you are, and use this to spur you on to achieve that dream.

"Find something you love enough to be able to take risks, jump over the hurdles and break through the brick walls that are always going to be placed in front of you. If you don't have that kind of feeling for what it is you're doing, you'll stop at the first giant hurdle."

– *George Lucas*

3. Myth Busting

MYTH: ALL THE TRULY ORIGINAL IDEAS HAVE ALREADY BEEN THOUGHT UP.

Nope. If that were so, science fiction authors would be out of a job! Artists, scientists, composers, inventors and a whole host of other creative people bring new ideas into the world all the time.

MYTH: IF SOMEONE KNOWS A LOT, OR GETS TOP GRADES, THEY MUST BE A GENIUS.

Not so. When he was 16 years old, Einstein attempted to enrol at the Swiss Federal Polytechnic in Zurich, but FAILED the entrance exam. He went on to study hard and get good grades at a school some 50km away, and was finally accepted at the Zurich Polytechnic when he was 17. Thankfully, anyone can learn to think more like Einstein, as we'll explore in the next chapter.

MYTH: BEING "SMART" WILL MAKE YOU HAPPY.

Afraid not. A good friend of mine who joined Mensa many years ago explained that it's actually quite depressing to believe that 99 out of every 100 people you meet have a lower IQ than you. It was disappointing to hear that so few members in that exclusive club were focussed on creating or inventing anything, but were instead spending their time solving puzzles and games.

However, if it is happiness you are looking for, I'm pleased to point you in the direction of Alain de Botton's book *'The Consolations of Philosophy'* which was also made into a six episode series, viewable online at: *www.alaindebotton.com/philosophy/watch/*

Alain does an excellent job of taking advice from some of history's greatest thinkers and making it incredibly easy to understand.

MYTH: CREATIVE THINKING IS LINKED TO IQ.

Not even close. Tests show conclusively that IQ has little to do with creative problem solving or originality of thought.

MYTH: ALL GENIUSES HAVE A HIGH IQ.

Not so. Howard Earl Gardner's *multiple intelligences* include: Linguistic, Logical-mathematical, Musical, Bodily-kinesthetic, Spatial, Interpersonal, and Intrapersonal. IQ tests do not measure every kind of intelligence. To obtain a high score you need to be able to think fast and focus on the task, that is, to be great at blocking out or ignoring non-relevant information.

What IQ tests DON'T do is weigh up the value or worthiness of a human being. Does a great composer, artist or poet have any less value in their contribution to society, just because they have an ordinary IQ score? Not at all.

> "Action is the real measure of intelligence."
> – *Napoleon Hill*

MYTH: ALBERT EINSTEIN'S IQ SCORE IS 160.

Nope. He was invited to sit IQ tests on several occasions, but he never took one. Perhaps he did not think very highly of them. So all of those news articles you see bandied about the place shouting out that a four year old child has the same IQ as Albert Einstein are nothing more than pure speculation.

MYTH: GENIUSES ARE BRILLIANT AT EVERYTHING.

Afraid not. Having known a few certifiable geniuses in my time, it is very reassuring to know that outside of their field of excellence, a genius will often make many of the same basic and 'stupid' mistakes as the rest of us. Thank goodness many are quite good humoured about it too!

> "Everyone's always going on about how thick
> David Beckham is. But nobody says:
> Stephen Hawking, shit at football - do they?"
> — *Steve Coogan*

MYTH: WE ONLY USE 10% OF OUR BRAIN.

We all need, and use, 100% of our brains - but not as effectively as we could be doing. Some would say that we only ever reach 10% of our true potential. From the 1890s, psychologist Boris Sidis accelerated his son's genius from birth, to reach an estimated IQ of 250-300 by age 11. Some of the techniques I'll be sharing with you a little later in this book will help you take advantage of the mysterious, 'hidden' part of the brain: the unconscious.

MYTH: I'M NOT THE CREATIVE TYPE.

Bollocks and rubbish! Everyone is BORN creative. We can all increase our levels of creativity. Sketching or doodling has been found to be an essential ingredient for creative and original thinking. If it's good enough for Leonardo da Vinci, it should be good enough for you.

MYTH: DRUGS HELP CREATIVITY.

Some artists are great in spite of their drug dependency, not because of it. Drug and alcohol abuse only delays the inevitable pain of sitting down and properly sorting out your issues. There are more **reliable** and healthier ways to get your unconscious mind working for you, such as ideation and creative techniques. Use these to reach your goals rather than risk messing up your life more than it already is.

MYTH: I NEED FANCY OR EXPENSIVE EQUIPMENT TO BE GREAT.

Nope. Renaissance artist Giotto was hired after drawing a circle. Yep, a PERFECT circle, free-hand, no tools. It was a simple, yet effective, demonstration of the focus and training of your mind with nothing more than your own hands, a pen and paper, or some chalk and a wall, or perhaps even a stick and some dirt.

On this topic, be sure to look up the finals of the World Freehand Circle Drawing Championship on youtube. It's possible Giotto used this particular technique, but we may never know for sure.

> "A man paints with his brains and not with his hands."
> – *Michelangelo*

MYTH: YOU NEED TO BE SOME KIND OF SUPERHERO.

Not so. Masterpieces, products or any other inventions don't instantly pop into your mind fully formed and perfect. Instead, ideas are worked over and over, like a dog chews away at a bone.

It starts out when the thought "this could be great", is mulled over, explored, played with, tested and refined. Whether the refinement is worked out on paper, as a series of prototypes, or purely as a mental exercise, does not matter. There are always snags and bumps along the way. Having the passion to see an idea through to the end is what's required - if it still fulfils a need.

On display at the National Maritime Museum in Greenwich London, are the H1, H2 and H3 prototypes of the world's first accurate 'sea watch.' Beside them is the revolutionary H4, constructed in 1759.

In the great Age of Sail, the H4 sea watch was used by the British for accurately measuring longitude, an essential ingredient for safe long-distance sea travel. If you can accurately pinpoint where you are with both longitude and latitude, like X and Y co-ordinates on a graph, you can also avoid the perils of shipwreck from previously charted underwater rocks and reefs. The British Empire's global expansion took off in a big way, because of the invention and use of the H4.

The H1, 2 and 3 are monstrously clunky and mysterious looking mechanical contraptions. In stark contrast to these is the H4. Next to its predecessors it seems like a giant leap of pure genius. It is instantly recognisable as a kind of oversized pocket watch. It's only after reading the exhibit captions that you discover the inventor, John Harrison, had a jeweller construct the H4 for him (unlike his previous models), and it was at this stage of his design process that he also chose to make it a more practical and portable item.

Many visitors to the exhibition mistakenly think the H4 was a great breakthrough because of the way it looks - its high quality finish - but the simple truth is that pocket watches had already been in use by wealthy Britons for almost a century and would have been familiar in its day. The *accuracy* of the new internal mechanism is what was remarkable, revolutionary, and key to its great success.

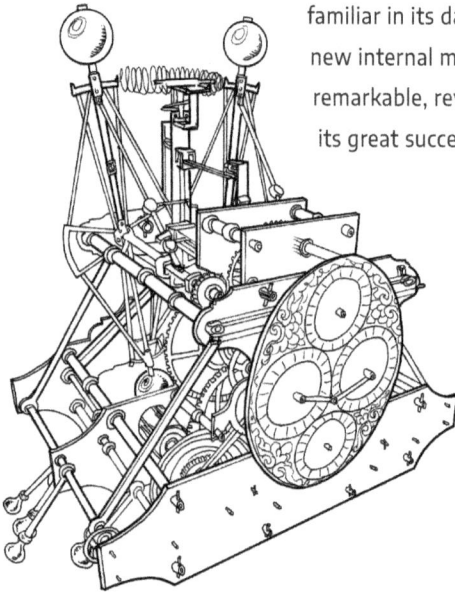

▲ *The H4 mechanism*

◀ *The H1 mechanism*

MYTH: A TIGHT DEADLINE GETS GREAT RESULTS.

Actually, stress is known to stifle creative thinking. Sure, you can come up with a solution in a few minutes or hours, but to come up with something truly brilliant, requires at least one night's sleep to ponder the problem properly. Use small milestones along the way for your project to help keep you on track and reduce stress later on.

MYTH: "THAT'S A GREAT IDEA"

Nine times out of ten, it isn't. Instead, push your thinking even further. Keep digging until you finally arrive at the 'wild ideas' part of your mind. Then, and only then, should you consider starting to judge your ideas.

MYTH: THE SELF MADE MILLIONAIRE.

> "How's that working out for you
> - being clever?"
> – *Tyler Durden, Fight Club film, 1999*

There are plenty of amazingly talented people in every town and city. You know the ones I'm talking about, their abilities are astonishing. Somehow they don't seem to make it to the big time, they struggle to get known. Why is that?

It turns out they are only *one skill short of success*.

Their missing link is either a mentor - someone who is already successful in what they're doing - or a great marketer who can get their message out there and keep getting it out there in the big wide world.

There is no such thing as a self-made millionaire, everyone needs some help. Just think about it.

Singers and songwriters need their marketing teams, studio producers, designers, editors, photographers, roadies and a host of other staff to help them. Even an author needs help for the layout and design of the book, printing, publishing, distribution and marketing of the book, before even a single penny rolls into their bank account.

4. Think Like a Genius

CURIOUS MINDS

If the nay-sayers of the world transformed their statements into questions, their minds would open up to a world of exciting new possibilities, instead of slamming the door shut on further thought. History's greatest inventions and ideas were brought about through enquiry, curiosity and imagination.

> "The person who says it cannot be done
> should not interrupt the one doing it."
> – *attributed to George Bernard Shaw*

> "The most expensive thing
> you will ever own is a closed mind."
> – *Anonymous*

CLOSED MINDS		CURIOUS MINDS
"I can't."	>>>	"How can I?"
"Why bother."	>>>	"Why not?"
"I can't afford that."	>>>	"How can I afford that?"
"What a crazy idea."	>>>	"Is it really such a crazy idea?"
"That's impossible."	>>>	"How can this be made possible?"

There is a gaping chasm between what we believe is impossible, and what can actually be achieved. As far back as 2,000 years ago, Seneca understood that the impossible is only made so by *a lack of trying*.

> "It is not because things are difficult that we do not dare;
> it is because we do not dare that things are difficult."
> – *Seneca, 1st century AD*

THINK LIKE EINSTEIN

Q: What's the difference between a patent office clerk and a Nobel Prize winning theoretical physicist?

A: About 20 years.

What really set Einstein apart was his curiosity, his willingness to ask *"What if...?"* What if the great Sir Isaac Newton was wrong about some of his assumptions behind his Laws of Motion? Einstein's proposal, that time is not constant, bordered on **heresy** as far as his peers were concerned. After all, they're called the **Laws** of motion, not

Theories, and they had stood undisputed for more than 200 years!

Einstein's theory was so radical it took years before it was broadly adopted by the wider scientific community. Some put this down to a generational shift - having to wait for the passing of senior scientists either unwilling or unable to change their thinking.

> "I believe in intuition and inspiration.
> **Imagination is more important** than knowledge.
> For knowledge is limited, whereas imagination encircles the
> entire world, stimulating progress, giving birth to evolution.
> It is, strictly speaking, a real factor in scientific research."
>
> *– Albert Einstein*

Take a moment to consider how stubbornly set in their beliefs they must have been, until Einstein proved them all wrong. They were blinded by what they *thought* they knew, by their knowledge. Curiosity and imagination open up many more opportunities than the 'known facts' ever will.

There is a media frenzy surrounding climate change news today. Where one would hope to find logic and reasoning, instead the news handles the topic in a way bordering on hysteria or religious fervour.

It is this limited, closed nature of the *debate* which I personally object to, rather than the subject or the truth of it.

> "I disapprove of what you say,
> but I will defend to the death your **right** to say it."
>
> *- Evelyn Beatrice Hall, on Voltaire*

A true scientific debate allows for opposing **evidence** to be considered, rather than relying on emotion or belief to dismiss all contrary views out of hand.

Are human activities really changing the climate or is it just naturally happening anyway? Only time, and scientific research, will tell. Since the Earth is currently the only home we have, logic tells us to protect what we have, that it is better to be safe than sorry. Whether the human effect on climate change is huge or tiny, we are responsible for it all the same.

The planet is a closed system, where what happens in one region can affect the rest. Governments everywhere need to replace those sources of energy which pollute the air, earth and water with harmless ones. It is an inherently worthwhile thing to do, since a cleaner environment is beneficial for everyone.

THE HALF-LIFE OF FACTS

Did you know that an enormous percentage of known 'facts' are found to be incorrect a few years later? For example, medical students are often told that around half of what they learn in college will be considered untrue, a mere ten years after learning it. Unfortunately you can never tell which facts will be the wrong ones.

In episode K07 (2013) of British television show QI, presenter Stephen Fry surprisingly awarded a bonus 737.66 points to panellist Alan Davies, as a kind of 'back pay' for answers given in previous episodes which had been considered wrong at the time. Stephen Fry announced that 60% of all facts in their first series of QI ten years earlier (**most** of the answers), had failed to stand the test of time.

WHY IMAGINATION IS MORE IMPORTANT

A few years ago the Chinese Government realised that, although their school system was producing great numbers of brilliant over-achievers, they were in desperate short supply of the home-grown inventors they needed for originating new products and technologies.

Chinese researchers looked to companies like Apple and Google, and found that the talented people who were coming up with great original ideas had something in common - they all read science fiction.

Thirty years ago, the Chinese saw science fiction as a kind of spiritual pollution from the West and it was all but stamped out.

Today, China is the world's biggest market for science fiction, with the opening ceremony of sci-fi conferences broadcast nationally.

> "Microsoft and Google, Apple and
> places like MIT are packed with
> science fiction readers and fantasy readers"
>
> – *Neil Gaiman*

START ASKING "WHAT IF...?"

To think like Einstein, follow your curiosity further than you ever have before. Don't put off discovering more about a topic. Google is a fantastic store of information and inspiration, but keep in mind that it is no substitute for coming up with your own original ideas. While researching to further your understanding, be sure to keep a healthy

dose of "What if...?" in the back of your mind.

Remember, Einstein's peers were all wrong in their assumptions, so what if everyone today is too?

"It's better to walk alone, than to walk with a crowd going in the wrong direction."

– *Diane Grant*

GIVE THANKS LIKE EINSTEIN

Be an enquiring mind about all things. Einstein realised every last little detail around him had been invented, or had originated from some past human thought. Be inspired by this simple fact, as Einstein was.

Look differently at the world you inhabit - all these fabricated objects which make up your office or home are the result of a grand collection of human minds throughout the centuries, each building on one anothers' ideas across time.

"A hundred times every day I remind myself that my inner and outer life depend on the labours of other men, living and dead, and that I must exert myself in order to give in the same measure as I have received and am still receiving."

– *Albert Einstein, The World As I See It*

Take for example the chair or stool.

It is an idea thought up thousands of years ago. The shape and sophistication have evolved, but the basic idea is the same. How might you personally invent a chair? What about a bicycle, or the paper clip?

How would you invent, from scratch, something radically different that performs the same task? What would it look like?

Thinking of the simplest, most familiar and humblest of creations in every home - inventions which have remained essentially unchanged for centuries - presents you with a great opportunity to invent a totally new solution.

IDENTIFY THE PROBLEM

First of all, you need to determine exactly what an existing item (solution) actually does. In this case, what does a chair actually do?

A chair is an object which keeps a person's rear off the ground while it is sat upon.

It must be sturdy enough to support their weight and should be of a size and scale to be useful.

Some have arm rests, others do not. It can be made out of many different kinds of materials, or a combination of materials.

What do you think of when I say "chair"?

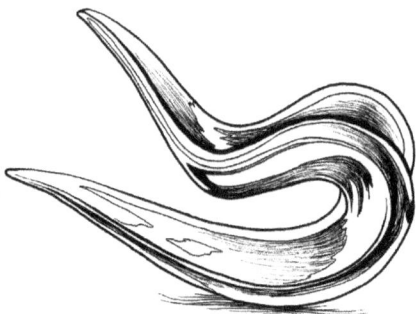

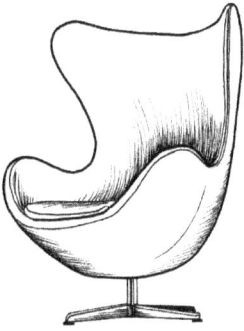

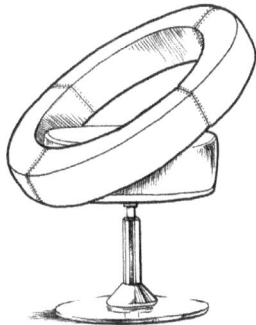

As you can see from the previous pages, there are many subcategories of chair as well: the stool, inflatable chair, rocking chair, throne, bench, swing and so on. Some chairs can be moved and still others are set permanently where they are, but they all perform essentially the same function.

The point of showing you this is to help you understand there are often many possible solutions to a problem. Will you drill down to the bare bones of a problem (which has a known solution), and push your thinking further than ever before, to arrive at a radically new solution?

We will explore methods to achieve exactly this, in a later chapter.

To ramp your thinking up to the next level, try identifying a hidden problem no-one's really considered yet, then ideate a variety of ways in which it might be solved. Look at it from new angles.

Don't know what I mean? Perhaps the following will inspire you:

FLYING IS IMPOSSIBLE, RIGHT?

Can humans fly? Ask anyone in the 19th century and they'd say you're crazy. After inviting the locals to witness the Wright brothers' historic first powered flight, five residents turned up and the rest petitioned to have them committed to an asylum. If you were invited to see a time machine in operation you might do the same.

Back in the day, everyone was in no doubt that people can't fly. They'd say: if God wanted us to fly we'd have wings. As it so happens, we have the imagination needed for dreaming up a contraption to help us do just that.

Consider for a moment that you're trying to build a safe and steerable flying machine before the Wright brothers had it all figured out. This is where you need to place your thinking to solve a new problem today. You need to **believe** that it can be solved.

> "When you want what you've never had,
> you must do something you've never done."
> – *Thomas Jefferson*

How did they do it? Without killing themselves, that is. The Wright brothers prepared to fail, frequently. They learned from their failures.

> "An optimist sees an opportunity in every calamity;
> a pessimist sees a calamity in every opportunity."
> – *Anonymous*

After finding a nice wide beach with constant wind for lift, and soft sand to minimise crash landings, they perfected their manual flying skills through hundreds of gliding flights.

The next step was to add an engine for sustained flight, but they could not find an engine which was both light enough and powerful enough for their needs. So they designed and built one themselves. And the rest, as they say, is history.

On a side note, even Nikola Tesla threw his hat into the ring, patenting a biplane theoretically capable of taking off vertically (VTOL) in 1928. He had invented the tiltrotor / tilt-wing concept as well as submitting the earliest proposal for the use of turbine engines in rotor aircraft. Way to go Tesla.

WHAT IS AN IDEA WORTH?

> "The single **greatest discovery** of my generation
> is that human beings can alter their lives
> by altering their attitudes of mind."
> – *William James*

Q: What does it cost you to come up with a great idea?
A: A slice of your time and the expenditure of some creative juices.

Consider what an idea is worth - to you; to the world. In 2012, the aviation industry globally was estimated to be worth more than $700 billion. Not bad for an industry based on something 'known' to be utterly IMPOSSIBLE only 100 years earlier.

UNASSISTED FLYING IS IMPOSSIBLE, RIGHT?

> "The Pessimist complains about the wind;
> the Optimist expects it to change;
> the Realist, adjusts the sails."
> – *William A Ward*

How does anyone really know what is, or is not, possible? All the wishful thinking in the world will not make me levitate while I sit here and flap my arms. Reality and experience tells me it is impossible. And right now it really is impossible!

Don't just sit back and blithely accept the status quo. No, you mustn't stop there. The biggest mistake we make is in giving up too soon. Begin by turning "It can't be done" into "How can it be done?" Take your thinking to the next level. Here we go, this should be fun....

"Reality is merely an illusion, albeit a very persistent one."
– *adapted from Albert Einstein*

Ideas that immediately leap to my mind are to either change the human body, or the mind. If you genetically alter the body, is the creation still really human anymore? At the very least the mind and consciousness would still be human.

Until now, gene editing was thought only possible in the **embryonic** stage. In 2014, a team of geneticists led by Daniel Anderson from MIT, successfully edited the genes of adult mice by injecting them with 'programmed cells' which act like a virus. They successfully reversed liver cancer in the **adult** mice.

This is the birth of an entirely new scientific field with incredible ramifications. Imagine receiving an injection one month, and growing wings the next. Incredible!

"If we knew what we were doing
it wouldn't be called research"
– *attributed to Einstein*

For altering or enhancing the mind, if I said 'telekinesis' I think every scientist and sceptic reading this book would wince or worse.

Interestingly though, we are now seeing some really promising advances in the use of brainwave harnessing gadgets such as brain-computer interfaces (BCIs) where participants are able to remotely control a computer using only the power of their mind.

In the 1930s, Nikola Tesla conceived of the Thought Camera, where thoughts would be projected on to a screen. Impossible? No, not at all. The technology for the Thought Camera is actually in its infancy today - how amazing!

Who knows? This kind of brain research, when combined with gene editing, could even bring about a form of unassisted telekinesis. Science fiction you say? Only for the moment.

Perhaps you can solve the age old problem of flight in yet another novel way, such as exploring how to go about creating localised anti-gravity fields or some such.

As they say, the sky is the limit - but only if you think it is. Einstein would approve.

TIME TO THINK DIFFERENT

Look at the simplest little things you take for granted every day, and ask yourself "why" is it so? How has this come to be?

> "The task is not so much to see what no one has yet seen,
> but to think what nobody yet has thought,
> about that which everybody sees."
>
> – *Arthur Schopenhauer*

Question all of your assumptions about the world around you. What do you think of as true? Do you consider something to be 100%

true because a trusted friend tells you so? They could be wrong, even though they've argued convincingly or passionately that what they say is fact. As the saying goes:

There is my truth, your truth, and the real truth somewhere in between.

Take a moment to consider what you KNOW to be true from your own personal experiences. Everything you hear on the News, from teachers and friends - how do you know if these things are true? You have trust and faith that these are truths, but that does not logically mean they are.

A magazine will say a few things about a celebrity, but do you personally know that celebrity?

No. Heck, you might never have laid eyes on them in the flesh, let alone chatted with them over coffee. 100% of the media is created by imperfect human beings who possess emotions and agendas. Unless you've personally spoken with people in every town and city, what you think of as your country is in reality interpreted for you by the media, teachers, parents and friends - and you weren't even aware of it.

A word of caution here. If you tend to form your opinions around emotion rather than logic, try adopting the opinions of logical thinkers you trust, until you can do it for yourself.

WE'RE ALL INDIVIDUALS (I'M NOT)

Most of us just go with the flow, even when we are 100% certain the crowd is wrong. The Asch Conformity Experiment confirms this.

In this 1950s experiment, the test subject is seated with a panel of four or five actors plus the organiser. Everyone's 'in on it' except the test subject themself.

It starts out innocently enough: participants are told to identify which of three vertical lines shown (A, B or C) are the same length as the one at left.

Each actor calls out their answer in turn, with the test subject sitting either last or next to last. A comfortable series of correct answers follows, and after a while the actors suddenly start calling out the exact same blatantly incorrect answer, one after the other.

How does our human guinea pig react to this? About 75% of test subjects gave an incorrect answer for at least one question during the session. In the control group, only 1% of all answers were incorrect.

They mainly cite one of two reasons: "There are four of them and only one of me;" (doubting their own answers) or "I knew they were wrong but why should I make waves?" (avoiding the pain of ridicule).

This instinct to stay silent and follow the crowd is closely related to that of survival. It is why we find it so hard to maintain our own points of view in the face of public opinion.

At investment events across the world, presenters describe wealthy investors as 'lone wolves' capable of spotting golden opportunities - which the rest of us either fail to see or fail to act upon. Then, having wooed the audience, all individuality goes out the window when told to run to the back of the room and part with $1,000's for the offered product. It is a great irony that the ones with this valuable lone wolf attitude are the ones still in their seats.

Why do we behave like this? Simple. We are afraid to go against the crowd, afraid of being cast out, afraid of being alone or unloved.

EINSTEIN'S COURAGE

> "Courage is the first of the human qualities
> because it is a quality which guarantees all the others."
> *– Sir Winston Churchill*

> "Embrace fear & it will loosen its grip on you."
> *– Philip McKernan*

Are you envious of the successful people you read about in magazines? The great achievers with their fast cars or high-flying lifestyles. Perhaps you are jealous of their courage? After all, they've mastered their fears long enough to take some pretty big risks and come out victorious on the other side. Good on them!

Did you know you can decide to stop fear and doubt ruling your life, ruling your decisions? The problem is it's much easier to fall back into easy, safe and comfortable habits you know, rather than face the risks of failure and embarrassment.

Get good at being uncomfortable.

Stop walking the path of least resistance.

> "Fortune is not on the side of the faint hearted."
> *- Sophocles, approx 400BC*

Einstein was brave enough to publish his theories, risking many years of ridicule. Taking on a scientific Law which had stood for over 200 years, sounds very much like trying to pull down a rock solid truth.

It just goes to show every 'fact' really is up for grabs - if you can prove it wrong. Had you been in Einstein's shoes, would you have been bold enough to say what no-one else was thinking?

THE PERILS OF OBEDIENCE

How about standing up to authority? Do you have the courage to stand up for what you know is right? Stanley Milgram, a young Jewish psychologist, ran an experiment to find out if ordinary Americans would blindly follow orders to the extent of committing murder.

The call for test subjects was put out in the guise of a study on memory. The unsuspecting volunteers were led by an actor in a lab coat to deliver a series of questions. They were instructed to administer an ever-increasing electric shock to the responder, for each incorrect answer given, with the last button said to deliver a fatal electric shock. The volunteer could talk with, and hear the screams of, the unseen actor pretending to be a test subject in the next room.

The actor in the lab coat was armed with a succession of verbal prods in this order: (1) Please continue, (2) The experiment requires that you continue, (3) It is absolutely essential that you continue, and (4) You have no other choice, you must go on.

The experiment returned devastating results: 65% of volunteers delivered that final, massive 450-volt shock - having been assured by some guy in a lab coat that they'll not be held responsible for murder.

Several participants are haunted to this very day, knowing they would have murdered someone begging them for mercy. As we are all responsible for our own actions, we must live with the consequences.

REBELLIOUS THINKING

> "It's more fun to be a pirate than to join the navy."
> *– Steve Jobs*

You've been trained at school to listen to and obey teachers and your parents; and to trust and believe in the authority of the news.

It's this constant habit of not thinking for yourself that fills you with doubt when finally you ask yourself: "is now the right time to break away, to swim against the tide?"

The world desperately needs more thinkers, more brave and original ideators - but where does this strength of courage come from?

> "It is easy to be brave from a safe distance."
> *– Aesop, 550BC*

Heroic acts are not performed by people who are fearless. Bravery springs from a deep desire to do what is necessary, what is right. It has its foundations in a deep sense of purpose and responsibility for your actions; in the rejection of all excuses.

Leaders stand up for the values they personally hold dear.

They suffer paralysing fear but choose to take action anyway. At those times when you find yourself tested in life, recognise your opportunity to step up and become a leader, to take action.

It is my hope that you'll realise how strong you are, more so than you ever dared to dream.

THE FUTURE

Ask a child what they think the world will look like 50 years from now. You may be surprised by their answers; blurted out with great energy, an optimistic outlook and an outrageous imagination.

Anyone can regain a childlike sense of wonder about the world by simply seeing the future through the eyes of the young.

The past holds lessons; the future holds possibilities.

SCHOOLING: A CASE STUDY

Speaking of the young, for the past decade Finland's school kids have rated amongst the best against other nations on PISA's tests, which weigh up the skills and knowledge of 15 year olds in 65 economies around the world.

The funny thing is, Finland's kids start school at age 7, have longer lunch breaks, shorter school hours and the smallest homework load of all industrial nations. There are almost no private schools and no gifted programs.

Are you confused yet?

In the 1960s, Finland made the decision to reform their education system, with the view that children are their country's greatest asset. The most obvious indicator of the new system's success is shown in a clear generational gap.

Results from the 2013 PIAAC survey, which tested 16-65 year olds, revealed that older Finns had only average abilities in literacy, numeracy and problem solving. In stark contrast, the younger adult Finns, who went through the new education system, had extremely high knowledge and strong know-how.

There are many reasons why the Finnish model works so well. It is a complex jigsaw of interrelated factors.

Here are just a few of them:

At the heart of the Finnish system lies an intense desire to develop the skills and talent of every child, with the mantra "we can't afford to waste a brain" commonly heard in staff rooms across the country.

> "Regardless of a person's gender,
> background, or social welfare status,
> everyone should have an equal chance
> to make the most of their skills.
> We are raising the potential of the
> entire human capital in Finland."
>
> *- Krista Kiuru, Finland's minister of education and science*

Teaching is a high-status job in Finland, requiring a master's degree plus ongoing training and support throughout their career. Teachers are valued and trusted to know what they are doing.

They are not tested so much as rather heavily supported.

'School shopping' is an alien concept because local schools are all as good as each other, no matter where you live. Even the universities are free.

By investing in their kids, Finland is investing in their future.

WHAT YOU CAN DO

Why not play devil's advocate (in a friendly and relaxed manner) with your friends and family so that they can also learn to play around with strange and interesting new ways to view the world we live in.

Entertain ridiculous notions because it is great fun! Daydream, play with ideas, follow your curiosity even further than you would ordinarily bother with.

Discover the great freedom and value of limitless thought - thinking without boundaries. Be more curious and questioning of 'the ways things are', than even the most annoyingly curious toddler!

Start thinking "What if...?" and "How can I?" instead of blindly accepting what you believe to be true. Is the world really round?** Do you personally know it to be true or is it yet another example of something taken on faith, because someone you trust or the media says it is so?

Question your every assumption and push the boundaries for what (you believe) is possible.

Beware your assumptions about people in authority. They are not always right, nor do they necessarily know what they're doing. Mahatma Gandhi led India to independence by coordinating national civil disobedience. Ordinary people stood up for what they believed was right against the ruling British authorities.

**Always remember that, just because you have made up your own mind about something, it does not logically mean you are correct (nor does it mean anyone else will want to hear your opinion).

Consider the half-life of facts: you may be proven wrong some time in the future.

5. You Are What You Think

I THINK I AM

In 2008, a study on creativity asked two groups to come up with as many uses for a brick as possible. The group exposed to the Apple logo at the start of their session came up with many more unusual and creative uses for a brick than those shown the IBM logo.

Why is this? Apple's *'Think Different'* campaign has built a strong link between their logo and the idea of thinking creatively. Just by looking at the Apple logo the study participants not only felt more creative but actually were.

The lesson to take away: when you believe you're creative, you actually become more creative.

Identify those triggers or scenarios that help you feel creative and run with it. Once you truly grasp the usefulness of a good self-fulfilling prophecy, you can purposely choose to take full advantage of it in all aspects of your life.

YOUR THOUGHTS ARE YOUR FUTURE

"Whether you think you can or you can't, you're right."

– Henry Ford

Author and real estate tycoon Robert Kiyosaki, highlights a phrase his mentor told him many times: "The word made flesh." Your thoughts and words reveal who you are and where you're headed. Words like "I'll never make that much money" or "I can't reach that goal" are only true because **you believe** they are.

Your words are your very own self fulfilling prophecy.

Hence, 'the word made flesh'.

"We give ourselves what we feel we deserve"

– Philip McKernan

ATTITUDE

Attitude is everything. If you believe there are crooks everywhere wanting to take away your hard earned cash, then that becomes your reality. It is what you look for - you constantly seek to validate your opinion of the world as 'the truth'. What you believe is what the world becomes, but only for you!

"We can complain because rose bushes have thorns,
or rejoice because thorn bushes have roses."

– Abraham Lincoln

The great news is you can choose what your outlook on life will be. Are your opinions a cage of your own making or do they set you free?

Believing the world is filled with great opportunities will help you hunt down solutions and, like every good self-fulfilling prophecy, raise your chances of success. By understanding this simple principle, anybody can change their attitude and the course of their future.

When blocked by an obstacle, see it as the perfect time to ideate - to think outside the box and come up with many ways to get around it.

"Remember that not getting what you want
is sometimes a wonderful stroke of luck."

– *Dalai Lama*

"I only got the opportunity to co-host a talk show
because I failed at news."

– *Oprah Winfrey*

WHAT DO YOU WISH FOR?

After blowing out the candles on their cake, children are told to keep their wish secret so that it may come true. There's a curious kind of logic in this. If you are told over and over that your outlandish dream will never come true, your dream will die before it has a chance to get off the ground. No little Jimmy, you will not invent a better space rocket. What a shame adults are such nay-sayers.

For many years as a child I wished for long-term happiness and wisdom. Now my secret is out in the open!

No, of course I had no idea how I was going to fulfil these goals, but in wishing for them I set the theme for my life - I am constantly on the look out for gems of wisdom. A lack of solutions **now** does not mean a lack of answers from ideation sessions in the future.

> "Most folks are about as happy as
> they make up their minds to be."
> – *Abraham Lincoln*

BECOME MORE SO

In his novel *'Dragon on a Pedestal'*, author Piers Anthony weaves the tale of an unfailingly optimistic little girl with the special ability to intensify the good which she alone can see in others.

After becoming separated from her minders, she wanders naïvely across the path of the most vilified creature in all the land. She finds a baby dragon, and with each exultation from the child of how strong, how brave and how wonderful the dragon is, **it becomes more so**.

> "Faith in oneself is the best and safest course."
> – *Michelangelo*

The story is sweet and poignant, giving us the touching example of a beautiful friendship which might never have happened due to prejudice. It is an allegory for setting aside assumptions, for love, forgiveness and **bolstering the self belief in others where they keep none for themselves**. What a precious gift.

KNOW THYSELF

> "Self trust is the first secret of success...
> the essence of heroism."
> – *Ralph Waldo Emerson*

Do you actually know what you really are, or are not, capable of? There are two, carefully balanced sides to 'Knowing Thyself' which can be summed up in these two questions:

Are you living in self denial? (e.g. "I will obey my diet" but you don't), and; Do you lack self belief? (e.g. "I can't lose weight" but you can).

I like to juggle these two sides of the coin with a mindset of what I call **introspective optimism**.

Introspective - to analyse where I am today and to spot where I might be lying to myself. Optimism - in looking to the future and knowing I'm actually capable of so much more than I might believe.

Another way of looking at it is in having your **head in the clouds** (working towards big dreams), but with your **feet on the ground** (keeping it real). Be hopeful, but not at the expense of reality.

SELF DECEPTION

> "You must never confuse faith that you will prevail in the end
> - which you can never afford to lose -
> with the discipline to confront the most brutal facts
> of your current reality, whatever it might be."
> – *US Admiral James Stockdale, Prisoner of War in Vietnam*

The problem with unchecked optimism is that you can lose touch with the reality of a situation.

An experiment on memory exposed participants to a range of statistics on the survival rates of diseases and other health related issues. When attempting to recall these depressing statistics, the 'optimistic' folk were too lenient, too optimistic in their guesses in comparison to the other participants. For them, the grisly reality just wasn't sinking in.

With obesity a real concern today, how many of us are far too optimistic about our future health?

Being overly optimistic might be why we don't commit ourselves to the weight-loss equation: energy in (food) needs to be less than energy out (physical activity). We simply fail to accept that an hour of hunger each day won't kill us, but a lack of exercise will.

A series of little steps (your bridge) make that big goal possible.

THE BEST KIND OF SELF DENIAL

Everyone lives in self denial of some kind or other. But is it always a negative? No. Here's the thing.

You can actually use self-denial to your advantage.

For example: why not 'fake it until you make it', by adopting a more light-hearted, innocent and trusting attitude? Of course, deep down you're still your usual savvy and untrusting self, but you soon find you're actually happier and less troubled.

That's making self denial work for you! That's using it as a tool to change your mindset and head in the direction you wish to grow.

THE POWER OF LABELS

In the 1960s, American school teacher Jane Elliott ran an experiment in an attempt to help her young students understand racism. She divided the class into blue- and brown-eyed students.

On the first day she assigned brown fabric collars to be worn by the 'inferior' brown eyed students.

Privileges were granted to the blue-eyed kids and they became more bossy and arrogant. Brown-eyes were told they weren't as smart because of the link between intelligence and blue melanin of the iris. The children's grades suddenly improved or slipped depending on which group they were in.

The following week, the roles were reversed, as were the behaviours, attitudes and grades.

You would hope the now 'superior' brown-eyes would have gained enough empathy to treat their opposite number kindly, but it was not to be so.

This experiment was later repeated, recorded and nationally televised, causing much debate and furore.

The lesson from this is to accept that you're as entitled to respectful treatment as the next person, regardless of your age, gender, sexuality, nationality, disability, intelligence, weight, faith or race.

Don't let those who look down at you rule your reality.

Don't think they're wrong; **_know_** they're wrong!

Get on with achieving your goals because you're not the problem, those who discriminate are the problem.

BREAK DOWN THE WALL

Never let being labelled hold you back, and never be blinded from seeing the true *spark and verve* of the person in front of you. They might be described as a disabled, deformed, childless, left-handed, atheist, jobless, drop-out, female foreigner.

But this exact same person could actually be an attractive, funny, successful, well-travelled, inspiring speaker, talented artist, singer, author, entrepreneur and well loved friend.

So don't be blinded by labels. Seek out the full flavour of their unique personality. There's potentially a beautiful friendship there, just waiting for you to uncover it. Be curious.

Smash down that wall of unfamiliarity. And never hold back your own dreams based on others' false ideas about who you are or what you're capable of.

STEREOTYPES

"Women are emotional and illogical creatures."

Whaaat?

Stereotypes are dangerous as they blind you to the reality of the person before you. It's just another way of labelling and discriminating. Both men and women can improve control over their emotions and their levels of patience (or anything else they choose, for that matter). Imagine controlling your expressions so well you could become a great poker player - such control can be hugely useful in other areas of your life. It's also pretty easy to learn logic and strategy skills, as there are lots of resources available to help you. Simply choose to dedicate your time and mental effort to learning.

With labels and stereotypes, beware adopting other people's flawed opinions. The same goes for listening to advice which would have you lower your own personal standards.

> "The minute you settle for less than you deserve,
> you get even less than you settled for."
>
> *– Maureen Dowd*

WALK TO THE BEAT OF YOUR OWN DRUM

Artists and writers are often told to make changes to their masterpieces, toning it down or diluting the message. Should they do it?

Agreeing to a deal means that both parties are satisfied with what they're getting. Unfortunately, when you're desperate you'll agree to almost anything. The best way to retain creative control over your work is to not need the money. A secondary income or an emergency fund to fall back on will help you keep control of your work and your future.

Shaw: Would you sleep with a man for a million pounds?

Fellow guest, roguishly: That depends on how good looking he was...

Shaw: How about for 10 shillings?

Fellow guest, horrified: What do you take me for?

Shaw: Madam, we have already settled that.
Now we are negotiating over price.

– George Bernard Shaw, terrorising a new dinner companion.

Walk to the beat of your own drum, not someone else's. Listen to what parents and others say, sure, but live a life of your own choosing.

You were born to follow your dreams, not to please others.

Set yourself good standards to live by, and be proud of your personal strengths. What if someone offered you billions of dollars to break your moral code? Would you rather lose money you're happy enough without, or lose your own self worth?

Watch out for those slippery slopes which take you further and further away from your own moral code, because you might just wake one day wondering where it all went so horribly wrong.

NEVER SAY NEVER

How do you know if something is really possible? Can all physical limitations be overcome? Never say never. If not today, it might be possible in the future.

Why not plan your bridge to make it happen? Can you change being too tall to qualify as an astronaut?

In an 'anything's possible' world, you would either change yourself or you change the rules.

Would you undergo surgery to lessen your height or could you change the rules through vast wealth (e.g. patronage) to build a larger space capsule? How would you become a pilot if you were colour-blind, or mix music without stereo hearing, or compete in able-bodied sport if you were a disabled athlete?

Just because you are told it's impossible does not make it so. Even Seneca knew the impossible is only made so by a ***lack of trying***.

WHAT YOU CAN DO

As mentioned earlier, adopt the mindset of ***introspective optimism*** with your ***head in the clouds*** (working towards big dreams), but with your ***feet on the ground*** (keeping it real).

Choose your attitude. If you are a bitter and resentful person, what makes you think you will live a happy, considered and enjoyable life? Watch how people you admire react to difficult situations and choose to emulate them. Learn to let go of those things which are a destructive force in your life, for your own health and happiness.

Think of all the different ways to react to a bully or unfair discrimination. You can choose to snarl back at them, to be angry and hurt. Or you can be at peace with the real truth of it - that you're not the problem, they are the problem.

Just because you believe something does NOT necessarily make it true. Always remember there is ***my truth***, ***your truth***, and the ***actual truth*** somewhere in between.

Food for thought:
Q: What is the difference between a terrorist and a freedom fighter?
A: The side reporting the story.

Above all else, live your own life.
And never, ever, lower your own personal standards for anyone.

6. Are You a Rat in a Cage?

Imagine you're living in a cage.

It's just the same metal bars holding you in the same place day after day. There's nothing new to do you've not already done a hundred times before. You're on your own with no-one else to chat or play with. Your life is painfully dull and you lose hope of ever escaping the cage.

And people wonder why depression is on the rise globally.

In-home entertainment is on the up and up, which means more of us are spending our precious time confined to the same four walls - our very own cage. When we go to work, we take the same route, and speak with the same people in the same office every day.

When you're stuck in a rut you're not getting enough of the mental stimulation you need.

Your happiness and mental health depends on variety. Perhaps that is one of the reasons it's known as the **spice of life**.

When was the last time that you did something for the first time?

There are two keys to a happy and healthy human mind.

The first is exercise, the second is **exposure to new experiences**. Exercise clears the debris out of your brain, carrying it away in the bloodstream.

New experiences keep life exciting.

These may include: meeting new people regularly, tasting new foods, learning a new musical instrument, visiting galleries and museums, or simply walking a different route every day for exercise.

When walking, take note of the different styles of architecture you walk past, or compare gardening ideas; whatever. Just make it your priority to get out and interact, share ideas and be inspired by others.

No ifs, no buts, just do it.

GET INSPIRED

On top of having brand new experiences, get some 'brain food' in your life.

Innovation magazines such as New Scientist can be a terrific source of exposure to other original thinkers. It's filled with radical ideas and future possibilities, all neatly set down in understandable language.

Alternately, both the *phys.org* and *iflscience.com* websites report on the latest breakthrough advances in the world of science.

The magazine Philosophy Now can also expose you to strange and interesting new ways of thinking.

Or you might take a leaf out of China's book and take up reading science fiction.

SEEKING HAPPINESS

> "The purpose of life
> is not to live it faster"
> – *Dalai Lama*

A study a few years back revealed that graphic designers produce their most creative work while they're in a happy and contented frame of mind. They enjoy the challenge of the task before them, their usefulness in life, and are not over-stressed. Creative thought is helped along by a playful and curious state of mind, rather than a panicked, stressed or flighty one.

So, with happiness being a key ingredient for creative thought, why are so many of us so useless at finding it? The smoking gun ironically lies at the feet of graphic designers and their bosses.

The 'noise' of advertising we are exposed to every day can be confusing. Advertisements purposely mix up images of friendship, family time, and enjoyment with their products or services knowing full well that most of us are confused about what makes us genuinely happy. They hope to trick us into thinking that our money can buy happiness at their shop.

Sadly, we fall for it over and over again.

We need to beware the advertisers' lure and focus instead on our true goal of happiness.

Why do we think others know what we need? Really, why?

The only person who really knows all the things that make your weird little heart happy is you!

> "Epicurus insisted that we only need
> three things to be happy – friends,
> freedom and an analysed life."
> *– Alain de Botton, Episode 2, 'A Guide to Happiness', 2000*
> *https://www.alaindebotton.com/philosophy/watch/*

Almost 2,000 years ago, a local councillor in a small town in south western Türkiye had a huge stone wall erected alongside the marketplace. Carved upon it were reminders of Epicurus' philosophy of happiness, for all the villagers to read while they shopped.

An excerpt from that wall reads:

> "Luxurious food and drinks in no way protect you from harm.
> Wealth beyond what is natural is no more use
> than an overflowing container.
> Real value is generated not by theatres and bars,
> perfumes and ointments, but by philosophy."
> *– Epicurus, approx 300BC*

It's almost unheard of for a politician today to go to such lengths. Can you imagine the objections from retailers if such a wall was proposed in a shopping mall today? You might think the wall was bad for trade, however, evidence among those ancient ruins points to a once-thriving and bustling marketplace while the wall and its message still stood.

It was nothing other than a friendly reminder that money cannot buy you the happiness or fulfilment you seek in this life.

BETTER, TOGETHER

There are countless examples throughout history where a gathering or hotspot of great thinkers shared their ideas, feeding each others' imaginations. Sharing and working on ideas together leads to a greater number, and better quality, of ideas for everyone.

It works for artists, writers, scientists, in fact any inventive field really.

Einstein and his friends set up their own club jokingly named the 'Olympia Academy.' In Oxford, the 'Inklings' meetings included noted authors CS Lewis (*Chronicles of Narnia*) and JRR Tolkein (*Lord of the Rings*). Rutherford and several of his students also shared their ideas, and each reaped their very own Nobel Prize.

> "Great things in business
> are never done by one person,
> they are done by a team of people."
> – *Steve Jobs*

The ultimate example is that great engine of ideas, the Italian Renaissance.

It was made possible by the great wealth of the Medici family in Florence. This is where the money was, and the Medici's were keen patrons of the arts and sciences.

Many of the most brilliant minds of the age gathered together to share their ideas: artists mixed with philosophers, musicians, mathematicians, astronomers, and so on.

The Renaissance was the birthing ground for the modern scientific age we enjoy today. So why not take inspiration from it and create or join your own club of diversely skilled people?

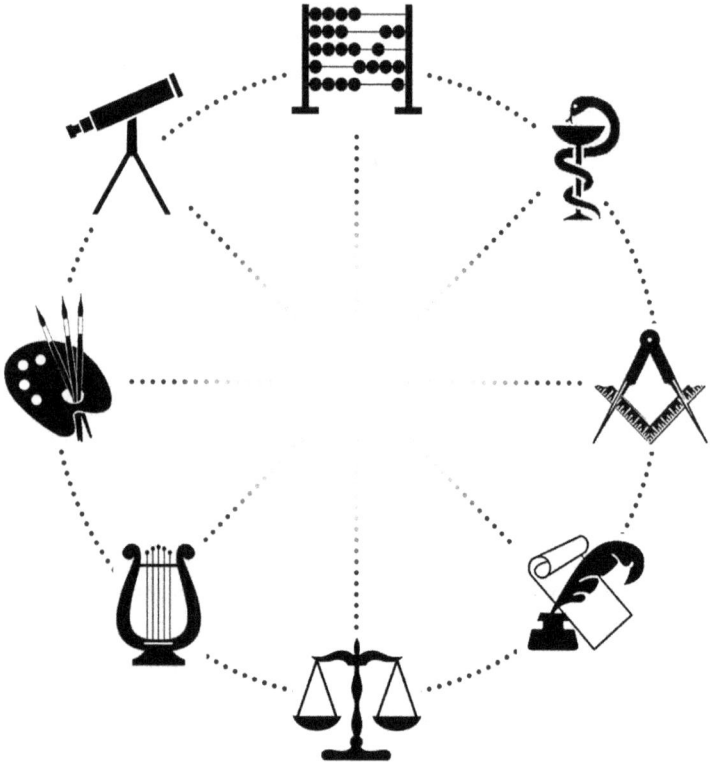

WHAT YOU CAN DO

Subscribe to thought-provoking magazines, blogs and websites.

You never know when or where inspiration will strike. So dedicate at least one evening per week to getting out and enjoying a new experience: make new friends, visit a gallery or museum, see a play, or taste strange new cuisine.

Think deeply about those times in your life when you were most happy and fulfilled. After reflecting on these past successes, remember how you arrived at them. Dream up and choose from an avalanche of exciting new challenges to achieve in the future. You could even ideate up new and unique ways to have fun, just for the thrill of it.

But be sure to savour the experience of ideation today, as it's an exciting experience in its own right.

Make your own little Renaissance. You could join a social club, hobby or networking group focussing on an activity or topic that captures your imagination. Even if it's a model train enthusiasts group, a 3D printer club, or scuba diving club it doesn't matter.

The friends and contacts you make now can lead to fantastic new directions in your future.

So what are you waiting for?

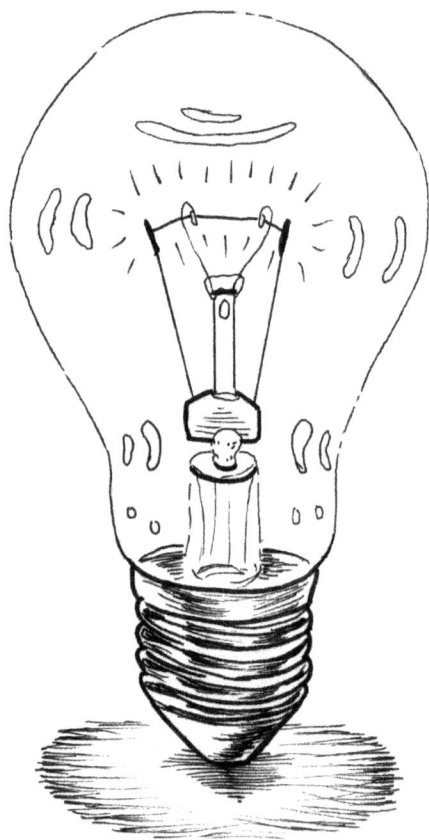

7. Boost Your Brilliance

Please consider the previous chapter as the first among the following tips on boosting your brilliance. These should aid you in the process of thinking and ideating. I have found many of these useful, but be sure to use the tips which you find work best for you. Enjoy!

NINE DOTS PUZZLE

Sometimes truly radical new ideas come from breaking the rules. The puzzle below was first published a century ago.

The challenge: *Connect the nine dots using up to four straight lines, without lifting your pen from the paper.*

The trick to solving this puzzle is to extend you lines past the edges of the box - hence, to '**think outside the box**.' The rules never said you couldn't, nor did they say your lines had to be only 0, 45 or 90 degrees in angle.

When you become more aware of your own assumptions - your **self-imposed** rules - you realise you can actually bend or break those rules. More choices bring about more creative possibilities!

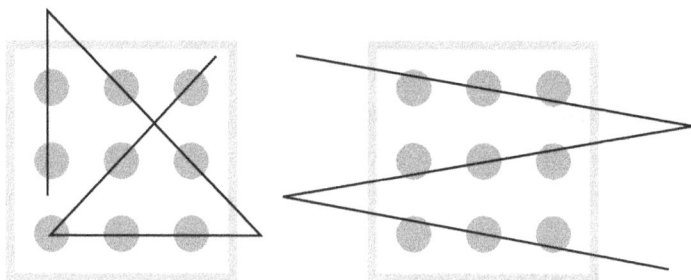

Above: Two possible solutions to the nine dots puzzle, thinking outside the box

INSPIRATION

When I'm stuck for inspiration with a deadline beating down on me, my two personal favourites are the Thesaurus and Google Images.

The Thesaurus is especially useful for reliably coming up with brilliant ideas for such things as a new company name, or drafting up a list of optional subtitles for the name of a new book.

Playing around with keywords on Google images is an excellent way of feeding your unconscious mind, giving it something to burble over before solving a problem.

SKETCH

How old were you when you gave up drawing? Don't worry about how bad you are at it, those stick figures are just fine. Doodling, or visual sketching, has been shown to help liberate creativity and memory recall when revising your notes.

In fact, a study by Professor Jackie Andrade found that 29% more of a rambling voice message can be recalled if you're doodling while listening, when compared with not doodling. If a picture is worth 1,000 words, a sketch must be worth a hundred at least.

The best example of a genius-doodler would have to be Leonardo da Vinci. Plenty of his doodles are vague little sketches made in three seconds or less. Just be sure to use unlined or unruled paper to keep your sketching free from constraint.

Kids are not afraid of their felt-tip pens, so why are you?

CLOSED AND OPEN MODES

Remember the Curious Minds section (page 44), where the statement "It can't be done" is turned around on itself as the question "How can it be done?"...

There are two essential ingredients for generating creative and original ideas: the closed and open modes of thinking.

The closed mode is factual, analytical, critical and serious. The open mode is imaginative, playful and questioning.

The open mode is used when the task at hand, the problem, is being considered from every possible angle, regardless of how whacky or seemingly random.

The closed mode is used to sort out the mediocre from the excellent ideas, analysing which will best fulfil your need.

After a round of idea filtering in the closed mode, pop back into open mode to explore your shortlisted ideas even further. Then go back into the closed mode for analysis and selection.

Both modes are absolutely essential for producing brilliant ideas.

PONDERING TIME

In my college days I was three quarters of the way through writing a 5,000 word essay when I misplaced it and couldn't for the life of me find it again.

After begging for some extra time, I started from scratch and worked late into the night to have it ready for the new deadline.

A few days later, I discovered what I'd done with my first draft. After the swearing died down, my curiosity got the better of me and I compared the old essay to my photocopy of the new one (I'd learnt the valuable lesson of keeping a back-up copy).

What I found is that the old essay paled in comparison to the rushed second version.

The new essay had only taken me about a third of the time to write, and it actually contained many more pertinent points than the first.

The reason for this?

Comedian and actor John Cleese refers to it as 'pondering time'. Others call it incubation time or soak time.

SLEEP ON IT

So, what is pondering time? It is the gentle yet persistent nudging against your unconscious, after you've already sat down and spent some time attempting to nut out the solution to your problem.

It's a bit like having an internal chat, telling your unconscious mind "come on brain, I know you're clever, you can pull a terrific solution out of thin air, be a good brain and come up with the goods by this time next week."

In the meantime, you think back to your problem at random times of the day and night, just quietly and gently reminding your unconscious about it, mulling it over.

Having spent enough time pondering the issue, your unconscious gets the hint that this is important enough to spend precious brain energy on. Low and behold, after a night or few of sleeping on it, the brilliant and obvious answer that was eluding you this whole time miraculously 'pops' to the front of your mind. Hurrah!

So do not worry about writer's block if you've first put in the pondering time. The ideas will come. Your problem might be to try shutting them off.

CAPTURE IT

Next comes preparing for the many odd and inconvenient times your great ideas will announce themselves to your waking mind.

I keep a notepad and pen by the bed, and have taught myself to write in the dark well enough to decipher it the next morning. I also keep paper and pens in my bag, in the living room and around my office. Sir Richard Branson often sings the praises of this one simple tip. Another idea is to keep a voice recording device handy everywhere you go.

For those times when you're in the shower or bath, you can write on sheets of non-stick baking paper/parchment on a plastic clipboard. Write using a glasochrom pencil, also known as wax, grease, or chinagraph pencils, or china markers. You can also write on dry surfaces like shiny tiles, mirrors or glass using a dry-erase (whiteboard) marker.

THE 5-10 MINUTE BREAK

Having set aside some quiet time to come up with ideas, you can still hit a wall of writer's block. To get yourself back on track, spend 5 to 10 minutes thinking about something completely unrelated. Stand up, walk around the room a couple of times, chat to a friend about their day. After a short break, you'll come back with renewed focus for the task at hand.

The same goes for those times you forget the important point you were about to make. If you discuss something else for 5 to 10 minutes, and try again to recall your idea, it will often pop suddenly to the front of your mind. Voila!

BRING IT BACK

You can recall an idea by retracing your steps. If you had a brilliant idea in the shower go back and try to remember what else you were thinking about at the time. It doesn't always work, but it's worth a try.

FAREWELL INSOMNIA

Aside from waking refreshed and feeling ready to face the day, sleep is an essential ingredient to health and happiness. While you sleep, your unconscious mind busily processes and squirrels away memories and learning from the day's activities.

Many sleep experts recommend you avoid doing homework in bed. Making a link between your bed (location) and work (activity) can interfere with your ability to drift off at bedtime.

Researchers all around the world have noticed a global rise in insomnia. Some hypothesise it's caused by the 24/7 nature of new information and our addiction to it - whether it's the 24 hour news or our social media feed. Actually, it might be caused by the devices we view our news on, stimulating the 'time to be awake now' sensors in our eyes.

Mobile phones and bright computer screens were directly linked to insomnia in a New Scientist magazine article a few years back.

The article revealed it is the blue hue of the light from these devices which mimics daylight and makes us much more wakeful, when compared to staring into warm yellow or orange hued lights.

In fact, most of the modern energy-saving light bulbs we use today give off a much harsher, blue hue than the incandescent bulbs of the past.

Not long after the New Scientist article was published, NASA committed to investing $11.4 million to replace the existing lighting on the International Space Station with new 'tuneable' lights to help astronauts sleep for longer than six hours at a time.

These new lights will offer astronauts the choice of blue or red hued lighting for use at different times of the day.

Luckily for the rest of us, energy-efficient bulbs are available in warm tones.

The *New Scientist* article I mentioned earlier recommended switching off monitors and mobile phones for at least an hour before bedtime and turning on gentle lighting around the home, such as table and floor lamps with light shades.

Here's to finally getting a good night's sleep!

K.I.S.S.

K.I.S.S. stands for Keep It Simple Stupid.

Nowhere is the spirit of this principle more closely embraced than at Apple, with their collection of easy to use technological products.

How did Apple come up with their apparently simple solutions in the first place?

> "If you can't explain it simply,
> you don't understand it well enough."
> – *attributed to Albert Einstein*

At the heart of the organisation is the strong desire to bring sleek products into the world, which are enjoyable and easy to use.

To achieve this aim, they carefully studied how babies learn.
If a toddler can use it and enjoy using it, then anyone can.

Much of Apple's success also comes down to the rejection of bad or merely adequate ideas (idea filtering), until you are only left with the very best and most simple of concepts.

"Simplicity is the ultimate sophistication."

– Steve Jobs

BE MORE NAÏVE

Try looking at problems from many different angles, such as looking at the world through a child's eyes, questioning every little thing. Try looking for a simple solution, because many problems do not need complicated solutions.

A wonderful example of this is the case of a truck or lorry getting wedged under a bridge it was too tall for. Many passersby suggest all sorts of solutions like cutting off the top of the truck, tearing the bridge apart, or ramming the truck out backwards with a larger vehicle. The more ideas to choose from, the better.

The best and simplest solution was suggested by a small child at the back of the crowd: why not just let the air out of the tyres?

Or then there's the example of a factory suffering a quality issue, where some boxes of toothpaste leave the premises empty. A team of engineers is brought in and six months later they install an obscenely expensive set of scales wired up to a bell which shuts down the assembly line every time an empty box is detected.

The tale goes that only a few weeks later there are no longer any empty boxes detected.

It turns out one of the factory workers had set up a $20 desk fan to blow the boxes off the belt and into a bin, as he was tired of having to walk over every time the bell rang.

REVERSE ENGINEERING

Think about an existing solution, then consider the problem that led to its invention. For example, the desktop fan might be the answer to staying cool while having both hands free. Something to replace a hand-held paper fan.

Here comes the fun part: imagine how the inventor would have gone about dreaming up the desktop fan. Think of all the other ideas they might have had.

Maybe your thinking will go down a totally different path, ending up with a solution that's just as good.

Of course, the fan is just one example.

Everything around you which fulfils a human need, and even the unobtrusive problems we are yet to recognise, offer up the chance for invention and new ideas. It's a great exercise in pushing your imagination further.

In his three part TV series 'Redesign my Brain', Todd Sampson introduces his audience to a word association game to increase creativity. This is a slightly different way to look at reverse engineering a problem.

It goes a bit like this: *object; verb+noun*.

For example, choose an object such as a paperclip.

The verb+noun that might apply to the object is "binds paper".

You've now laid bare in the simplest terms, the problem which the paperclip solves - it binds paper together.

The final part of the exercise is to list off as many other items as you can, that solve the same problem. For example: stapler, sticky tape, glue, binder and so on.

Playing this game every day will boost your creativity and problem solving skills.

VISUALISATION

Did you know you can increase your dart throwing skills without even picking up a dart? In the same TV series, Todd's skills were assessed in two sessions of darts, each a month apart. During the intervening four weeks, he spent a few minutes every day with his eyes closed, visualising himself successfully throwing the dart into the middle of the target every time. When he finally did pick up a dart for the first time a month later, his score was vastly improved.

The thing to be wary of with visualisation is to avoid negatives.

For example if I say to you "do NOT think of a chair right now" your unconscious will have instantly produced an image of a chair for you.

A member of my family likes to play a trick on the fourth hole at the local St Lucia Golf Course. He tells his fellow golfers, "Wow look at the size of those trees, and they're right in the middle of the fairway too. You really want to miss those trees, they're so huge."

Unsurprisingly, they suddenly act like huge magnets sucking in the golf balls like magic. His own ball of course sails majestically down to the distant green, having focussed his attention on precisely where he wants it to land. Knowing this tip, I wonder when Google will change their company motto away from "Don't be evil."

Keep in mind that before meeting your favourite author, if you tell yourself "Don't go all fanboy and don't embarrass yourself" you will probably go all fanboy and embarrass yourself. And then you'll wonder why it happened. Trust me, I know...

A much more useful thought would be: "Remain calm and be professional. You'll leave a great impression because you're awesome".

SOLVE WORLD POVERTY IN 5 MINUTES

Everyone knows not to expect a workable solution to world poverty in such a ridiculously short space of time.

By using a statement that is unbelievable if not downright ridiculous, you're actually taking away the stress of performance anxiety.

This means the participants in this group warm-up activity can just relax and have some fun with it. The fear of saying something silly is silenced, leaving everyone ready to limber up their creative juices. There are many other great techniques to 'stretch-up' before an ideation session. I personally recommend '*Thinkertoys*' by Michael Michalko to discover many more.

EXTREME PRACTICE

Futsal is a five-a-side variant on football which is played indoors, but on a smaller and hard surfaced field, and with a less bouncy and smaller ball. Generally speaking the skills needed to rise to the top in

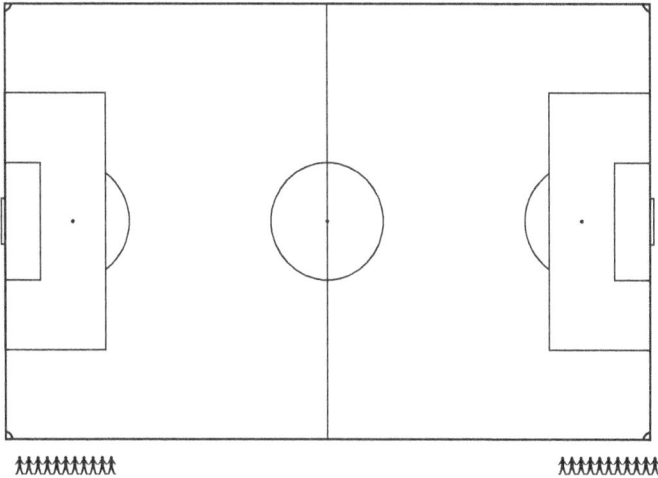

♀♀♀♀♀♀♀♀♀♀   ♀♀♀♀♀♀♀♀♀♀

Comparison of field size.   Scale: 1:1,000
Above: Association football, international field
Right: Futsal court

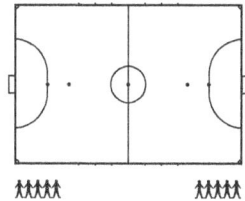

futsal are more finely honed than those
needed for regular football. More people
in Brazil play futsal than football.

During their rise to global dominance, the Brazilian football team
trained regularly at futsal while wearing weights on their legs.

When it came time to play football, the players felt light and quick
on their feet without the weights, the ball was bouncier, the field was
enormous and grassy, in fact everything felt much easier in 'live' play
than during their practice sessions. This gave them a huge advantage
over their opponents.

The lesson here: extreme practice leads to easy performance.

EMPATHY

> "That would be a good idea."
>
> *– Mahatma Gandhi,*
> *when asked what he thought of modern civilisation.*

Empathy is another great ingredient for creative thought. Imagining yourself in someone else's shoes is an excellent way to view the world from a totally different perspective.

When imagining you are someone else, you consider which of the many past events in their life story are most likely to influence the decisions they make about their future. By understanding what motivates someone, what their unresolved "chip on the shoulder" issues might be, you can more accurately ***predict*** their future path.

But what can people predict about you? After reviewing your own past you start to see why you make certain decisions. Being mindful of this can help you avoid repetition of your past mistakes.

Another great way to look at an issue from all angles is to answer these six questions: ***who***, ***what***, ***when***, ***where***, ***how*** and ***why***?

For example: Who will use this product? What are they using instead? What else do those sorts of people like? When will they use it and where? Where and how do they most like to shop? How will they hear about my product? Why is this product not already available, or is it?

The more questions you pose, the more the problem is explored and better understood, and the more possible solutions you will come up with to eventually choose from. More ideas mean more chances to find the best possible solution.

AIM HIGHER

Why not aim to be as good as (or better than) the best in your field? Find out what is required to achieve this, and commit to doing whatever it takes to become that expert.

We'll explore this further in Chapter 8 'Death to Mediocrity'.

ADD A LIMITATION

It may seem counter-intuitive, but adding a limitation can lead to more creative ideas.

It's part of defining the problem that needs to be solved. If you were to task someone with fixing all the world's problems they wouldn't even know where to begin. If instead you present a very specific task, the ideas will flow as if on cue.

Imagine you're part of a team of people tasked with generating ideas for a new car advertisement. After a few false starts, an arbitrary limitation of "horror genre" is set on the session, and suddenly a floodgate of weird and wonderful ideas gushes forth. It is not that the team lacks creativity, but simply that the task was not well enough defined in the first place. So take the time to define your challenge.

Here's an example of adding a limitation for a (scandalously) creative outcome. When challenged to produce a sentence including the word 'horticulture', Dorothy Parker famously replied with a twist on the old proverb about horses and water:

"You can lead a horticulture, but you cannot make her think."

Good ideas

Great ideas

8. Death to Mediocrity

"The enemy of a Great life is a Good life"

– Jim Collins

ENTERTAINED TO DEATH

What price a distracted life? Are you living your life to its fullest or are you only whiling away your time? Will you look back on your life and think "I've achieved" or will you say "I was properly distracted"?

Most of us don't bother with creative thinking or inventing.

The choice you face is to remain a consumer all your life, or to become a creator instead. Recognise your habits of procrastination, stop putting things off to another day, and decide to get stuck in now rather than later. What if later never comes? Will you be a good example for the next generation or will you **pass the buck**, saying in your own defence that your kids are your legacy?

A great way to get motivated and make a start is to ask yourself WIIFM: What's In It For Me?

What would just one brilliant and original idea be worth to you in your lifetime? How about a dozen?

You owe it to yourself to live up to your potential while you still can.

BE UNIQUE

Sometimes being the odd one out can be your lucky break.

That, and turning up.

Australian actor Mel Gibson got his big career break when he landed the starring role for the first '*Mad Max*' film. He fronted up to the audition all beaten up and black-eyed from a pub brawl the night before. He'd just made the casting agents' job easy. They didn't need to imagine the rough and tumble character they were looking for - here he was right in front of them.

Hollywood's first true child star, Shirley Temple, was chosen out of countless little ballerinas when she was just four years old.

As the other girls were lining up for inspection at the dance studio, Shirley ran and hid behind the piano. She caught the eye of the visiting talent scout, and the rest is history.

MOST IDEAS ARE BAD IDEAS

> "For brilliant ideas to live, good ideas must die."
> – *Hugh MacLeod, author of 'Ignore Everybody'*

Most ideas are either bad or merely adequate. The first dozen or so ideas from a 'cognitive dump' or ideation session are often unoriginal ones, floating at the top layer of your unconscious.

To find the truly original ideas, you first need to get the junk out of the way - the ideas that float about at the top of your thoughts - and keep digging down until you strike the crazy-wild ideas.

Allowing off-beat and seemingly irrelevant (bad) ideas to flow forth can often prompt and lead to the genius ideas you've been searching for.

Just keep going. When you chew over a problem, gnaw away at it persistently like a dog chews on a bone. Expect the mild unease that comes with having not yet solved a problem, we all feel that. Simply put up with this unease longer than others would, and you'll soon discover what a terrific source of 'creativity on demand' you can be.

Creative ideation is about as close to having a real magic wand as we can get.

Trust in your unconscious mind. It is much much more clever than you are, but is a bit lazy and needs the extra prompting and frequent reminders (made by you) to get on with spitting out something original.

"Nearly every man who develops an idea works it up to the point where it looks impossible, and then he gets discouraged. That's **not** the place to become discouraged."

– Thomas Edison

"I'm actually as proud of the things we haven't done as the things I have done. Innovation is saying ***no*** to 1,000 things."

– Steve Jobs

HEED YOUR UNCONSCIOUS

Have a look at the inside front cover of this book.

These two pages show repositioned magnifications (300%) of my greatest masterpiece. It's shown at 70% scale at right. It was intended to be so similar to the old celtic style that it would be inconspicuous when placed amongst the pages of the great Books of Kells or Durrow.

A pet hate of mine is the misguided belief that if you whack a celtic knotwork border around some calligraphy, you can call it celtic art. Banish the thought! This project was for me the single most challenging artwork of my life.

Why? Well, it's not simply a case of copying something. No, I was making it all up from scratch. Once I was satisfied with the 'big picture' shaping and overall layout (can you read the word *KNOW* at right?), I suddenly realised I needed to invent a calamity of tiny whorls and intricate knots to fill up the endless unique spaces I had just created. Again, this is something that cannot simply be copied.

I had some crazy-weird dreams during the painting phase. It seemed the image of the page was burned onto the back of my retinas. In my dreams I observed one of the small whorls in the corner rotating on the spot in a clockwise direction. After a moment or two, the two adjacent whorls kicked off in an anti-clockwise spin. Then, slowly but surely, the whole scene sprung to life, like a series of cogs in some Victorian genius' great invention.

When I awoke the next morning, I was curious to discover if such a spin/direction rule exists in the ancient illuminations I was studying. Yes, in fact I did discover patterns to the direction of spin, so my

unconscious had helped me make sense of the whorls I was studying.

All great artists know when to heed warnings from their unconscious mind. The painting stage alone took me an entire month to complete. This is because I could only paint for two or three hours each day before a little niggle of worry crept into my mind telling me I was about to ruin it.

I had learned many years earlier that ignoring such warnings from the unconscious almost always ended with the artwork getting smudged, a paintbrush accidentally dropping on it, or otherwise ruining it in some fashion or other.

When you're on a roll, fine, keep at it. But stop when uncertainty strikes, or you will doubtless suffer an unhappy self-fulfilling prophecy. Don't give up! Be determined to reach your goal in spite of setbacks.

NEVER REST ON YOUR LAURELS

After an intensive drawing workshop, a class of art students were sent home to finish their super-real cross-hatch drawing. The next day, the finished drawings were put up on the wall for critique and assessment.

The results were spectacular. Some students had put in six or seven hours to complete their artwork. After assessment, the students were required to burn the drawings, and to destroy any photos or photocopies of the artwork. There was to be no record at all of their efforts.

> "If you want to live your life in a creative way,
> as an artist, you have to not look back too much.
> You have to be willing to take whatever you've done
> and whoever you were and throw them away."
>
> – *Steve Jobs*

Although heartbreaking, the lesson is a vital one: **never** rest on your laurels. Most of all, don't buy into the hype that your own artwork needs to be distanced and worshipped behind glass. It is a personal thing, made with your own two hands. You must always look to the future for what you will create next.

The same goes for any inventive field: you're only as good as your latest thing. Keep going.

You don't want one or two ideas, but plenty and often.

KICK OUT THE YES-MEN

'Yes-men' love to agree with everything you say without hesitation. It seems too many politicians and too many CEOs listen to the advice of yes-men, who only reflect their opinions back at them. Surrounding yourself with yes-men can make it almost impossible to get an honest opinion, just when you need it the most.

Some of the friendships I hold dearest are with my devil's advocate friends. They respectfully ask tough questions such as "Why would you do that?" or "Why do you think that?" They're the ones who challenge me on my most basic assumptions about the world, and make me analyse the reasons behind why I hold certain opinions.

They ask these questions for the love of a good debate, and to explore topics in depth and from many different angles.

Listen to the advice of others, but always make up your own mind. Listen carefully to your critics and customers. They are telling you how you might improve, and they're doing it for free!

They're your greatest source of honest feedback - you'll never get that from a 'yes-man'. They don't contribute anything new.

> "Sir, I have tested your machine.
> It adds a new terror to life
> and makes death a long-felt want."
>
> – *Sir Herbert Beerbohm Tree, 1853-1917,*
> *on an early predecessor of the record player.*

One company doing a terrific job of acting on advice is Adobe, who produce Photoshop and Acrobat amongst other things. Their bottom line has gone from strength to strength, because they continually improve their products after listening to feedback from their loyal fans, their customers.

WHAT COST, POOR ADVICE?

How do you separate good advice from poor advice? One way is to look at who's giving it. Would you ask a yo-yo dieter how to lose weight? Would you expect top quality advice from an expensive but experienced lawyer, or from your friend's cousin who's just graduated?

> "Nothing kills your great ideas more than people with small ideas and limited imaginations."
> – *Robert Kiyosaki*

Would you rather take financial advice from an employee or from a rags-to-riches millionaire?

Don't know any millionaires? How about experts, philosophers or others you think highly of? Nope? Sounds like an excuse to me.

Who says you can't go meet some? Remember, if you don't ask, you don't get. The worst that can happen is they tell you they're too busy. So try a different tactic next time. How about using the *law of reciprocity*: give them a personalised gift and ask if they'd mind having a chat over coffee at a time that's convenient to them. Remember, there's got to be something in it for them to give you their valuable time.

SELF DOUBT

> "Doubt kills more dreams than failure ever will"
> *– Suzy Kassem, 'Rise Up and Salute the Sun'*

Bringing your dream to life is the single most exciting, pinch-me experience you can ever have. You suddenly know how Alice felt going down that rabbit hole. You think to yourself "Oh my goodness, what am I doing?" and you panic. Have faith in your well thought-out plan, and take comfort that you are headed in the right direction.

> "Usually the biggest demon is not out there.
> It's what's inside your head."
> *– Rick Hansen*

Even presidents first stepping into their office - stepping quite literally into history - experience what is known as the Imposter Syndrome. They are riddled with self doubt, with terrible uncertainty. They think: who am I to be making such important decisions? Anyone finding themselves in a position of responsibility can handle their doubt by following the maxim: fake it 'til you make it. Or better still, until you become it. Carry on, gradually growing into the role until you discover a few weeks later you feel like you really belong.

> "[Believing in yourself] is like being in love.
> No-one can tell you you're in love,
> you just know it, through and through."
> *– Adapted from The Oracle, The Matrix film, 1999*

"Beware; I am fearless, and therefore powerful."
– *Mary Shelley*

If you think further about it, what is a president other than a man or woman? They were a child once; they might even have been bullied at school. They are not super-heroes, they are simply a person with many skills and abilities that they've chosen to hone.

If they can step up to a great challenge, why not you?

"There is nothing in the caterpillar that tells you
it's going to be a butterfly."
– *Buckminster Fuller*

DREAM BIG

"While you're already thinking, why not think really BIG?"
– *American saying*

Most of us limit ourselves to a small dream, because we believe a big dream is beyond our reach. And you know, if that's what we think, then that is exactly what we'll get and nothing more. How sad.

"The greatest danger for most of us is not that our aim is too
high and we miss it, but that it is **too low** and we reach it."
– *Michelangelo*

Take a good look at your most far-fetched and ambitious dream.

You need to look at your end goal and ask yourself "How can I do this?" rather than stating "I couldn't possibly do this, not in a million years." When you ask "How can I do this?" you start to play around with all sorts of ideas. You can then move forward, breaking it down into little steps along the path.

Build your bridge between today and the future, across to where your big goal sits on the far side waving back at you.

Your bridge, your plan, your actions all combine as the only way to bring your dream out of the shadows and into reality.

> "We choose to go to the moon in this decade
> and do the other things. Not because they are easy,
> but because they are hard."
>
> *– John F Kennedy*

BEST PRACTICE

The Romans were masters of implementing best practice. Arguably their greatest strength was their policy of stealing the best ideas from each culture they encountered and adopting it right across the Empire. Out with the old, and in with the new improved ways.

Companies today which miss opportunities to innovate are finding themselves left behind in a ruthlessly tough and competitive market. So why not make like the Romans: if there's a better way, do it.

> "Good ideas almost never overcome your competition. Because
> the 'other guys' are going to do WILD (ideas). Bet on it."
>
> *– C. McNair Wilson, author 'HATCH!'*

THE PARETO PRINCIPLE

Also known as the 80-20 rule, the Pareto Principle states that about 80% of effects come from 20% of causes. For example, in business 80% of your sales come from just 20% of your clients. Once you identify which clients they are, you can focus on ensuring you keep them happy.

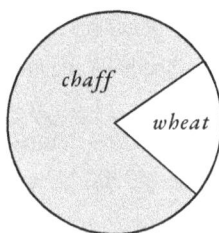

The principle works in many different areas: 80% of crimes are committed by 20% of criminals; 80% of health resources are used by 20% of the patients, and so on.

The 80-20 rule can be very handy for increasing personal effectiveness at work. Consider paying someone else to do those tasks which are necessary but tedious, which bring in the least income compared to your other tasks. That way you can just work to your strengths. You'll be free to spend more of your day focussing on the 20% of tasks which do give you the majority of your income.

> "Focus on better use of your best weapons
> instead of constant repair."
>
> – *Tim Ferriss*

QUALITY

What's the secret ingredient of Apple's success? Pure and simple: quality. Countless thousands of proposals were ideated, analysed, sorted and rejected until only the very best concepts remained.

> "Quality is more important than quantity.
> One home run is much better than two doubles."
>
> *– Steve Jobs*

> "If you refuse to accept anything but the best,
> you very often get it."
>
> *– Robin Sharma*

Never settle for anything less than the best from yourself. Who knows how much you are actually capable of achieving? One thing's for certain: when you hold back from fulfilling your potential, the only person you're cheating is yourself.

> "If we did all the things we are capable of,
> we would literally astound ourselves."
>
> *– Thomas Edison*

> "If you knew how much work went into it,
> you wouldn't call it genius."
>
> *– Michelangelo*

JUST BECAUSE YOU CAN,
DOESN'T MEAN YOU SHOULD

The headline above is one of my favourite sayings, highlighting that *not every idea is always a good one.* I wish I had a dollar for every time I heard someone say "I know, we could get Jen to photoshop...."

Sigh. When I hear those words, the saying above instantly runs through my head.

The best example of this theme I've seen in recent times is a succinct little meme popping up on social media sites reading:

SCIENCE can tell you
> **_HOW_ to clone a Tyrannosaurus Rex.**
HUMANITIES can tell you
> **_WHY_ this might be a _BAD Idea._**

The meme finishes off with a fun picture of a T-Rex about to eat the scientist who created it!

WHAT YOU CAN DO

If you don't want your gravestone reading "....was entertained to death" take action. Start by switching off the telly, closing down Facebook, and get creating and inventing instead.

Don't just stop at the first one or two good ideas, since great ones may be just a few short minutes away, buried just under the surface of the next layer in your unconscious.

Only you can dig 'em up and set 'em free.

Adopt the attitude: you're only as good as your latest thing. This will keep you fresh, keep you current and keep you moving onwards to bigger, brighter and better things!

Appreciate genuine and honest feedback. It is much more valuable than kind words from loved ones, because it's harder to come by and contains free lessons for doing a better job next time.

Tackle fear and self doubt: Fake it 'til you make it.

Actions speak louder than words - don't just dream it, do it.

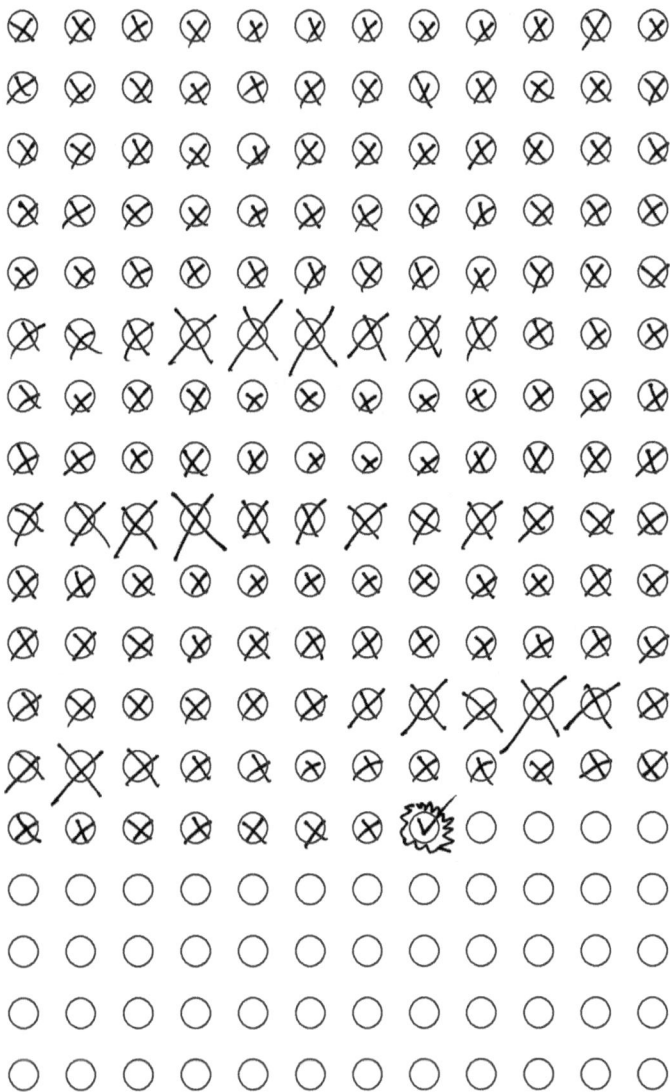

9. Shirts of Iron

> "Habit is a shirt of Iron"
>
> – *Slovenian proverb*

Q: Why are most New Year's Eve resolutions broken within the first two months?

A: Because it is much easier to fall back into old habits.

Those bad habits which we already have are so immovable, so binding, we feel unable to move forward. It's as though we are imprisoned in shirts made of iron. As mentioned earlier, rather than trying to break habits, it is much easier to dissolve them away gradually until they're replaced by new ones we really want.

> "We are what we repeatedly do.
> Greatness therefore is not an act but a habit."
>
> – *Aristotle*

Our minds are amazingly malleable and adaptable to learning new things. If you choose to convince yourself that learning is both fun and easy, it will actually become true for you. It's all down to attitude and self-belief.

Thankfully, coming up with great ideas gets easier the more you do it.

Just like when you build up muscle, those weights are darned heavy at first, but the more you do it the easier it gets. And so it is with forming the new habits you'll use for original thinking.

> "We cannot become what we want to be
> by remaining what we are."
> – *Max DePree*

CHANGE OVER TIME

Here's the thing about change - it lowers our happiness factor when we first begin. Change feels unfamiliar and uncomfortable.

Take a look at the chart below.

Now, take the example of moving house. When you first move in

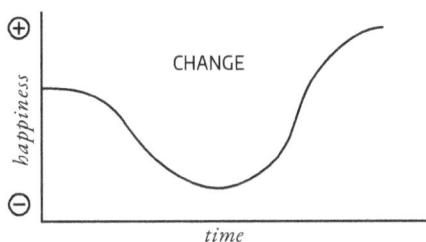

it's super exciting, but soon you take note of all the little things that aren't quite right about the place. The taps that drip, a gate that doesn't stay shut, or mice getting into the kitchen.

By the time each niggling little problem is fixed, happiness levels will have bounced back to their previous state and continue on to a new high.

This chart can be used for many other instances of change as well, such as when staff need to learn how to use a new system at work.

If you genuinely wish to become more creative, more brilliant, or more 'anything' really, by definition you need to change away from who you already are.

> "He who cannot change
> the very fabric of his thought
> will never be able to change reality,
> and will never, therefore,
> make any progress."
>
> *– Anwar Sadat*

Give up who you used to be, and learn new ways of doing things.

Are you the same person you were 10 years ago? No, you have grown and learned many things, you've been influenced by the world and have different opinions now than you once did.

Thinking and ideating need to become your new 'normal'. They need to become embedded into your everyday thinking, to become a new part of who you are.

Decide who you want to be - take control of your own re-invention.

YOUR JOB

> "I am the Captain of my soul."
>
> *– Nelson Mandela, quoting from William Ernest Henley's 'Invictus'*

Looking after your future is not the government's job, not your boss' job, nor anyone else's. It is your job.

You are the captain steering your own ship, mistress or master of your own destiny. Words such as "I don't want to" or "I don't feel like it" shows a lack of care for the consequences. They are words you'd expect to hear from a child, not a responsible adult.

Of course, life will throw random events across your path, but you can choose how you deal with it. Will you think of yourself as an unfortunate victim of fate - or will you pick yourself up and rise to the top against all the odds? Learn to rise above this cruel, cruel world.

> "To forget one's purpose is the
> commonest form of stupidity."
>
> *– Friedrich Nietzsche*

THERE'S NO JUSTICE, THERE'S JUST US

Injustices happen in every town in every country, because the world is not a fair place. Stop thinking it is, and instead start ideating all the ways which you might improve or change your life.

Successful entrepreneurs know that the world owes them nothing. To learn this lesson, delegates at a workshop on entrepreneurship were split into groups of three and set a one-hour task to come up with a campaign slogan and poster for a proposed product.

The delegates knew their efforts would be critiqued and count towards 10% of their overall score for the weekend. When their time was up, each group presented and explained why their slogans and posters should work - why their ideas were the best.

The trainer had other ideas. He gave everyone a truly dreadful score. Some he gave 3 out of 10, others only 1. After arguing with him, one group scored zero. He almost had a riot on his hands!

After calming everyone down, he reminded them the weighting was only 10%. He also hammered home his point that the market is brutal. It seriously does not care how hard you worked on your proposal, or if you really meant to say something else on your poster. If they don't like it, they will not buy it - simple as that.

Entrepreneurs already know 'fair' does not enter into the picture where the market is concerned. But they also know to keep on trying to find new ways to do business, and see opportunities others miss.

LEARN FROM FAILURE

> "Success is the ability to go from one failure to another with no loss of enthusiasm"
> – *attributed to Sir Winston Churchill*

A little girl went ice-skating with her father. After falling down all night, almost in tears, she told her daddy what a failure she was.

"You watched me fall down all night" she said.

Her father replied "That's not true, I saw you keep on getting up."

> "Why do we fall Bruce?
> So we can **learn** to pick ourselves up."
> – *Bruce Wayne's father, Batman Begins, 2005*

Years of schooling has conditioned us to avoid making mistakes, but it's how we learn life's greatest lessons. Be honest with yourself, and put your failures into perspective. Use them as guideposts on how to succeed the next time around.

Don't be so afraid to make mistakes that you never start anything. Work past your fears and take action.

If you secretly think it's too big a project to do all on your own - then don't. Get help by partnering up with someone you trust, or find yourself a good mentor. Just don't give up - your turn will come.

> "He who never made a mistake
> never made a discovery."
> – *Samuel Smiles*

THE NUMBERS GAME

How many times can you handle rejection before giving up? Five? Twenty? How about 1,000 times? The founder of KFC, Colonel Sanders, was 65 years old when fate threw a huge spanner in his works. He suddenly found himself penniless, forced to close his restaurant when a new highway diverted most of his customers elsewhere.

> "When nothing goes right, go left."
> "If at first you don't succeed, try a different way."

Keeping in mind that male life expectancy in the US was only 67 years back then, Sanders was determined to start up his very own fast food franchise. Incredibly, he spent two long years on the road, tirelessly canvassing to restauranteurs about his franchise.

He was rejected not 10 times, 100 times, 500 times, but a staggering 1,009 times before eventually finding his first 'yes'.

Failure was not an acceptable option for him.

He had faith in his business model and was driven to succeed. Imagine going through the pain of rejection so many times. Could you keep picking yourself up again when everyone keeps telling you 'no'? Success really is, after all, just a numbers game.

"I haven't failed, I've found 10,000 ways that don't work."
– Thomas Edison

When cooking up a batch of hot ideas KEEP GOING. Don't judge or evaluate as you go along, but leave that to the closed mode later on. Let the ideas flow because a bunch of half-baked or bad ideas can often lead to the real gems.

"The best way to have a good idea is to have lots of ideas."
– Linus Pauling, Chemist and Nobel Prize winner

NEVER; NEVER; NEVER

Sir Winston Churchill's steely resolve led Britain to victory against Germany in World War II. The country seemed terribly alone and poorly armed against the might of their enemy.

Churchill delivered many tough and gritty speeches. He had faith in his people's ability to 'grin and bear it' - that in focussing on long term goals, through thick and thin, they could methodically work their way through to eventual victory.

And so they did. Steely determination won the war.

> "I have nothing to offer but blood, toil, tears and sweat...
> What is our aim? Victory at all costs, victory in spite of
> all terror; victory, however long and hard the road may be,
> for without victory, there is no survival."
> – *Sir Winston Churchill*

Next time you feel yourself giving up, consider Churchill's words on the next page. Revisit your original goals and the reasons you set out on this path in the first place.

If the reasons are still valid, work to renew your passion and resolve then and there to find a way to reach your goal.

Hurdles will always cross your path, but these are **opportunities** in disguise - opportunities to overcome, to succeed where others have given up.

> "These are not dark days; these are great days
> — the greatest days our country has ever lived."
> – *Sir Winston Churchill*

View the problem from all angles, ask others for their ideas, research, search for inspiration - but above all else, never give up.

WHAT YOU CAN DO

TAKE ACTION, create good habits and never give up!

"Never give in, **never give in,**
never; never; never; never
- in nothing, great or small, large or petty -
never give in except to convictions
of honour and good sense."
– *Sir Winston Churchill*

10. Bonus: How to Change the World

"When I was young and free and my imagination had no limits, I dreamed of changing the world.

As I grew older and wiser, I realised the world would not change. And I decided to shorten my sights somewhat and change only my country. But it too seemed immovable.

As I entered my twilight years, in one last desperate attempt, I sought to change only my family, those closest to me; but alas they would have none of it.

And now here I lie in my death bed and realise, perhaps for the first time, that if only I had changed *myself* first, then by example I may have influenced my family and with their encouragement and support I may have bettered my country, and who knows, I may have changed the world."

– attributed to an Anglo-Saxon Bishop, circa 1100 AD

"Yesterday is history.
Tomorrow is a mystery.
Today is a gift.
That's why it is called the present."

– *Alice Morse Earle*

11. What Next?

As all good things must come to an end, so too have we come to the end of this book. It is my hope that you've enjoyed reading it and have garnered lots of great techniques, tips and tricks to take away with you - helping you arrive at brilliant "eureka" moments more often and more reliably.

I hope to someday hear of the difference this has made in your life, and of all the wonderful new ideas you have brought to the world.

If I were to condense this book into a few words I would say:

Be positive, stay curious, ask "What if...?", make your own luck, be inspired (but sleep on it), be brave, follow your dreams and above all else never, ever give up.

Change yourself to change the world. Be the change you wish to see.

Start living an extraordinary life today. You can do it!

"Have the courage to follow your heart and intuition. They somehow already know what you truly want to become."

– Steve Jobs

Thanks for reading,
I hope you enjoyed it!

WHAT YOU CAN DO

Who do you know, who'd also really enjoy reading this book? Do them a favour and tell them all about it, or better yet, share the love by gifting them a copy.

Reviews can go a long way in supporting the authors you love, so feel free to leave an honest review at *Goodreads* or *Amazon*. It'll help spread the word, and let more people discover and be inspired by this book.

Why not follow your curiosity and discover what else Fraser has been working on lately?

To find out more about her latest projects, inventions and offerings visit **bio.site/jenfraser**.

Or hire her to speak: **hello@jen-fraser.com**

My most brilliant idea, so far

Continued from page 5. (chapter 1)

A few years ago I made several of the techniques in this book a regular, day-to-day part of my life. My efforts were rewarded by having personally come up with a major scientific, award-winning idea.

Sadly for me, I was about 30 years too late! The idea had already been discovered, tested and accepted as theory.

My idea was that the Earth, spinning like a child's spinning top, experiences a minor wobble on a regular schedule (say, every 10,000 years or so for example), creating a predictable cycle of mini ice ages lasting about three to four hundred years.

Here's how I arrived at this idea:

Climate change features heavily in mainstream media today, and in exploring my curiosity around the topic, I decided to search for clues in the past for predicting our future. Although Art and English - not Science - were my strongest subjects in school, I thought to myself: "Heck, ***why not***, this could be fun."

While living in London, I learned of the severe 'Little Ice Age' Europe had experienced between around 1500 and 1850. It was so cold that wool merchants' fortunes were made seemingly overnight, and the Mercers Livery Company became the most wealthy and powerful of the London City Guilds, on the back of the booming wool trade.

In Scotland, families were evicted in their thousands by greedy landlords keen to use the land for grazing sheep. The mighty River Thames froze over so thick that an elephant was able to be led across the ice, walking from one bank to the other. The river played host to many great Frost Fairs and festivals during the 350 year period.

However, what really piqued my curiosity is that there are earlier signs (literally) of pleasantly warm times in London with street names including Vineyard Close and Vine Street. What could be affecting the climate so? The London I know has very mild and stable weather. I decided to think more deeply about what causes **our most predictable and regular climate changes,** the cyclical four seasons.

The seasons are opposite in the northern and southern hemispheres. They are caused by the Earth's tilt as it spins in its orbit around the Sun. During our annual (365 day) journey around the Sun, we experience summers when the tilt of our own hemisphere is closest to the Sun and winters when it is tilted furthest away.

If the Earth had **no lean at all**, both hemispheres would have the same seasons at the same time. We'd have seasons caused by the elliptical shape of our orbit. If you think about it, we would have **two** summers and **two** winters every year.

So what would happen if today's Earth **with its current lean** experienced a little wobble? A more extreme lean would mean more

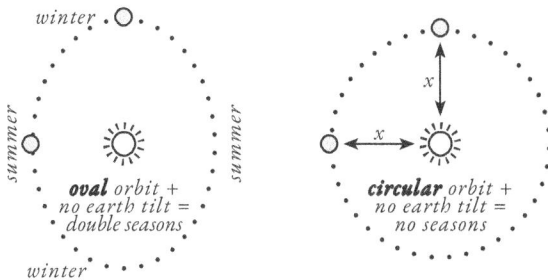

winter

summer

summer

oval *orbit +*
no earth tilt =
double seasons

winter

x

circular *orbit +*
no earth tilt =
no seasons

x

extreme seasons, with a more upright axis resulting in milder seasons. Could such a wobble last for years, and perhaps even centuries, thus causing mini Ice Ages? The answer is yes.

I had discovered Axial and Apsidal precessions - two of the ideas behind Milankovitch cycles - which cause changes in our climate including Ice Ages. It's the amount of heat from the sun that affects our climate the most, and solar activity plays its part in this as well.

Milankovitch cycles calculate that the Earth experiences a wobble roughly every 42,000 years, and this theory was backed up by evidence from deep ocean core samples in 1976. Although the Little Ice Age mentioned earlier doesn't line up with these cycles (which were most likely caused by increased solar or volcanic activity) it kicked off my curiosity and got me thinking about it in the first place.

Milankovič has been ranked among the top fifteen minds of all time in the field of earth sciences. There is even an award named in his honour - the Milankovitch Medal. Of course the greatest difference between Milankovič and myself is that he devoted many years of his life to exploring his idea, including calculating the length of these heavenly cycles. Clearly, I have not. My hat is off to him!

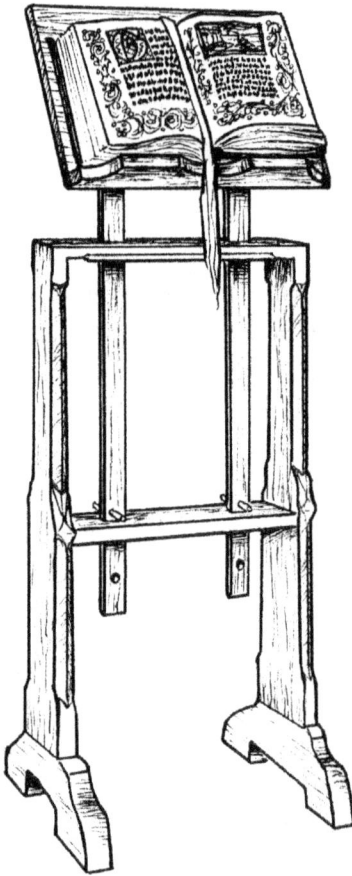

Bibliography

Bird, J 2006, *How to Change Your Life in 7 Steps*, Vermilion, London

de Botton, A 2000, *Philosophy: A Guide to Happiness. (2000)*. Episode 2, Epicurus on Happiness, ABC, Australia.

Einstein, A 2006, *The World As I See It*, Citadel Press, New York

Heilbroner, R 2000, *The Worldly Philosophers*, 7th Edition, Penguin Books, London

Hill, N 2007, *Think and Grow Rich*, Wilder Publications, Radford, VA

Imber, A 2009, *The Creativity Formula*, Liminal Press, Caulfield Victoria

Kiyosaki, R & Lechter, S L 2002, *Retire Young, Retire Rich*, Time Warner Paperbacks, London

MacLeod, H 2009, *Ignore Everybody*, Portfolio, London

Mattimore, B W 2012, *Idea Stormers*, Jossey-Bass, San Francisco, CA

Michalko, M 2006, *Thinkertoys*, 2nd Edition, Ten Speed Press, New York

Miller, P & Wedell-Wedellsborg, T 2013, *Innovation as Usual*, Harvard Business Review Press, Boston

Sampson, T 2000, *Redesign my Brain (2013)*. Series 1, Episode 2, Make Me Creative, ABC, Australia.

Wilson, C McNair 2012, *HATCH!*, Book Villages, Colorado Springs USA

Thanks

The author wishes to acknowledge the Jagera and Turrbal peoples, who are the traditional custodians of the land where this work was created. She wishes to express her respect for their tribal elders, to celebrate the tremendous strength of their continuing culture, and to acknowledge the memory of their ancestors.

This book would never have come to pass without the encouragement and assistance of many fine people.

To Judeth Wilson of Upfront Communications, thank you for suggesting that I had a book's worth of things to say, just begging to be put into print. Judeth, you were right!

Thanks to Yvette Blanchard for the timely and honest feedback on the first draft, which led to the first major re-write.

To my sister Kathy, I'm so grateful for your input early on, the final proof-read, and for your vote of confidence in the finished product.

I'm pleased to credit her husband, Malcolm, with being so brilliantly entertaining that I simply had to include four of his stories in this book!

A spot of fact-checking by Jenny McSaveney was both timely and well appreciated, many thanks.

I'd also like to express my heartfelt gratitude to Kate Haddock for her meticulous work on the legal side of things, prior to publication of this work.

A huge wave of gratitude to the many reviewers and praisers of the book, and most especially to Piers Anthony for his entertaining foreword.

And lastly, to my husband Steve. Thank you for providing essential guidance for the final major re-write. Thanks for all of your support, patience, honest advice and encouragement. Most of all, thank you for just being you.

Index

jen-fraser.com

About
the
Author

Originality Trainer & Speaker

JEN FRASER

Helping ambitious professionals
discover the magic of bold ideas
via *originality* training.

jen-fraser.com

JEN✱FRASER

The Magic of *Bold Ideas*

Jen Fraser is on a mission to unlock human ingenuity...

Through her unique approach, audiences learn how to discover bold, original ideas; so they can finally thrive — not just survive.

Award-winning author and illustrator of '*Everyone's a Genius*', Fraser brings to the stage a well-crafted fusion of humour, inspiration and thought-provoking revelations.

As a patent-pending inventor, with a successful 15+ year former career in creative design, she draws on a wealth of captivating stories and life experiences to inspire and inform audiences.

Fraser is an Adobe Certified Expert (ACE), and holds a Certificate IV in Training and Assessment (TAE40110). She currently resides in Ipswich, Australia.

jen-fraser.com + www.outthinx.com

Copy Cat

— 1ST EDITION —

HOW TO Escape Status Quo Thinking & Lead THE Field

Award-Winning Author & Inventor
by **JEN FRASER**

Buy Now at:

www.outthinx.com/shop

.